Susan   'colleagu

to buy -   ....   you

enjoy

            George

FLYING, FARMING AND POLITICS:
A LIBERAL LIFE

GEORGE MACKIE

Flying, Farming and Politics:
a liberal life

LORD MACKIE OF BENSHIE
CBE, DSO, DFC, LLD

The Memoir Club

First published in 2004 by
The Memoir Club
Stanhope Old Hall
Stanhope
Weardale
County Durham

British Library Cataloguing in
Publication Data.
A catalogue record for this book
is available from the
British Library.

ISBN: 1 84104 094 0

Typeset by George Wishart & Associates, Whitley Bay.
Printed by CPI Bath.

For my granddaughters
Clementine, Sunnifa, Jessica, Arabella,
Hannah, Isabella and Lizzie Lindsay

Contents

List of Illustrations

Foreword

THE MACKIES OF ABERDEENSHIRE are an extraordinary family, and George an extraordinary member of it. He gave me my first job on graduating in 1962: £895 a year as Assistant Secretary to the Scottish Liberal Party. The job was supposed to last a year, but since the election was delayed to the last minute in 1964 it lasted two years, during which, as he recounts, he was instrumental in moving me to fight in the Borders. Thus began my entire career; so writing this foreword is an ultra-modest recompense.

George is always blunt and to the point as this volume testifies. I can add two memorable examples from the early sixties. He decided that three of his young candidates in hopeful seats needed some basic education in agriculture. Thus Russell Johnston (Inverness), John Mackay (Argyll) and I (Roxburgh, Selkirk & Peebles) were summoned to a day on his farm at Benshie, where we were royally entertained to drink and food by him and Lindsay and taken on a lecture tour of the farm where we tried to grasp the intricacies of the subsidy system and other basics of the agricultural industry. It was a hugely enjoyable day, but Mackie reported to the Executive that 'Johnston and Steel were absolutely hopeless; Mackay was quite good'. Johnston and Steel were in due course elected by their more discerning constituents, while Mackay was not, and duly left to pursue a reasonable career in the Tories.

The second occasion was during a by-election in a badly organised rural constituency with a sound and worthy but rather diffident, shy and unconfident candidate. Big George came to speak at a meeting and next morning take him round the local mart on auction day. The farming crowd welcomed him as a noted figure in their world and were less impressed by the little man he was trying to enthuse over. After an hour or so we were making our way back to the campaign office when the candidate said: 'Mr Mackie, did you think the speech I made last night was OK?' I can picture the scene still: an exasperated George turned slowly to him in the street and declared: 'What you said was perfectly good, but if I may give you some advice – since you ask – it would help if when you are speaking you did not hop from one foot to the other as though you had just shat your breeks.' The poor man went on to lose his deposit.

This memoir does more than encapsulate George Mackie's remarkable life, it gives us pen pictures without frills or flourish of life in pre-war rural Scotland, of wartime in the RAF, of political and commercial struggles, and of worldwide travels. At each stage he tells it as it was, with humanity and humour. It will bring joy to many.

The Right Honourable Lord Steel of Aikwood KBE PC DL

November 2003

CHAPTER 1

My Forebears

FOR WELL OVER 300 years my forebears on both sides were farmers in Aberdeenshire, mostly in the hard country of Buchan. There, they played their full part in the taming of that countryside described by Dr Johnson as 'a blasted heath'. They were hardy men and even hardier women, and I am proud of them.

My maternal great-grandfather was tenant of Mains of Fedderate, New Deer, which he leased in 1820 as a 70-acre farm, taking in a further 100 acres in a lease of 19 years. My paternal grandfather, John Mackie, was extremely able and he was, I suppose, one of the first multiple farmers. He put all his five sons into farms, helped by the fact that they inherited some from their grandfather Leask of Skilmafilly. He married twice and the second family were in fact more cousins of ours than uncles as they were approximately the same age.

John Mackie was a hard but fair master and a man of a good deal of wit. He had several flocks of sheep, which he wintered on other people's ground, renting their keep on grass before Christmas and on turnips thereafter. An old shepherd of his told me that on one occasion he had his flock on turnips up beside New Pitsligo and the day before he would finish the turnips, he was waiting for my grandfather, to see where he had to take his flock next. My grandfather appeared in his gig and said, 'Well, Willum. Have ye got keep for the sheep?' Willum replied, 'No. Hiv ye?' My grandfather took five shillings out of his pocket, handed them to Willum, and explained: 'That's the keep for the sheep for ten days, after which I have turnips taken. Until then you must drive them along the roadsides slowly and they will eat the uncropped grass – the five shillings is 3*d.* a day for your dinner and 3*d.* for a pint of porter.' This would obviously have been said in broad Doric – I have translated!

Once, I was told, he complained to his grieve – the farm boss – that the dung was not being driven fast enough out of the midden. The grieve replied that they needed an extra man to load the carts. My grandfather said that at yoking time, one o'clock, there would be an

1

extra man. The grieve was waiting at one o'clock: my grandfather appeared with a chair and a newspaper and sat himself down by the midden. Sure enough, in the evening the number of loads driven was satisfactory to my grandfather, who then asked his grieve, 'Were you pleased with your extra man?'

An old cattleman, Geordie More, whom I had the good luck to know when I was a boy, told me many stories of my grandfather, whom he had served. A not so nice tale was that of a cattleman who did not please him. One morning he went into the byre, pointed out several faults, and when the cattleman fired up and said, 'You can sort your cattle yourself!', the old man opened his hand and there was his wage packet.

Geordie had numerous stories of the farming life in those days. All the men would be assembled at the turnip singling. They would be in a long line with a drill apiece, the foreman in front and the last row brought up by the grieve. It was a time of great chat and Geordie More was in his place near the end of the line. One of the men had been in the Boer War and he was telling a long tale about a skirmish. He was being pompous and boring. Eventually he came to the highlight and said, 'We had the Boers surrounded and suddenly the order came to cease fire. Dae you ken why?' Geordie More piped up in a weary voice, 'Aye. You were feared they would turn on ye.'

The stories about the life of my other grandfather, who was an auctioneer as well as a farmer, are rather different. An old friend of my father's told me that, when selling the furniture at any roup, his comments were not only funny and kept the audience going but were also invariably extremely coarse. He had a mare called Rattlin' Jean, of which he was exceptionally proud, and he once bet his cronies at the market in New Deer that he could travel the hilly road to Methlick without reins and without traces. He set off followed by a large crowd of spectators and successfully arrived at Grant's Shop in Methlick by skilful manipulation of his weight on the gig, pressing on the shafts through the saddle, and word of mouth to his favourite mare. The party then continued at Grant's Shop which acted as the local inn. He died quite young, at the age of 70.

My father, Maitland Mackie, was a remarkable man. As was often the case in farming families, he was meant to be a doctor, but on completing his schooling at age 18 at Aberdeen Grammar School, he returned home, threw his books in the corner and said, 'I want to be a farmer!' My grandfather replied, 'Ah well, laddie. We will maybe get a farm to you some day.' He went to work on Mains of Elrick until my grandfather took a very nice farm, Milton of Noth, Rhynie, and sent my father up there to be in charge while he prepared to move. So at the age of 19 he was in charge of a 300 acre arable farm lying at the bottom of the hills, with 3,000 acres of hill behind. He greatly enjoyed the mixture of arable and hill farming and I think regretted it when his father came up to take over.

Maitland was then sent down to North Ythsie, an out farm of my grandfather's, to take over there. North Ythsie is a good arable farm of 370 acres in the district of Formartine, about 17 miles from Aberdeen in the Parish of Tarves. He was to die there in 1975. In 1909 or thereby, he rented another farm, Westerton, Rothienorman, and applied to the bank for some money to take this farm. The banker was not a manager, but the agent, a farmer and merchant called William Duthie. When approached by my father, he said, 'Carry on, Maitland. I will gi'e you a' the money you want!' Different days.

One day my father was going by gig from North Ythsie to see his father at Milton of Noth, a distance of some 30 miles. It was a very cold day and when he got to Pitcaple, he stopped the gig at the merchant's and called for a gill – a quarter of a pint – of whisky. He drank it straight down. When told that whisky actually lowers the body temperature, his reply was, 'It might have been a great delusion on my part, but I was warm all the way to Milton.'

His next farm was Thomastown. There he started dairying, selling the milk in the small nearby town of Huntly. Shortly thereafter he got the farm of Easterton, which adjoined Westerton – making a unit of 700 odd acres. He also took a small sheep farm near Thomastown called Denend. I was sometimes rather worried as a small boy that he had not been in the First War as so many other fathers had been, for he was in a reserved occupation. He must have been greatly helped by the good prices during the War. After it, my uncle, George Yull, who had taken over my mother's family farm of Little Ardo, went to Australia and my father took over the lease, buying that farm also.

He was an admirable organiser, who had his budget firmly down on the back of an envelope and the work organised on each farm, so that the maximum use was made of every hour of labour. He also had the advantages of scale and bought all his fertiliser at one go from whichever company gave him the best terms. During the bad times between the wars, Thomastown, in dairying, returned £1,000 a year, while the other farms made or lost a little money. Quite early on, he started a flock of breeding hens on Little Ardo and this farm did produce reasonable profits of £600 or £700 a year. By 1935 he had decided to convert all the farms to dairying, and did so over the next few years.

He helped a very large number of people. A neighbour called James McNaughton, known as Jimmy Nachty, had a small farm next door where he lived with his sister. He had been a sergeant in the Gordons in the First War and came back to some years of prosperity in his small farm. Being a social character, he spent that which he had. When the bad times came, he found he could not pay his rent. My father was approached and did all the business, doling out a small allowance to James, while he put the enterprise back on its feet. James was grateful and every Christmas brought my father the biggest of the turkeys which his sister reared for pocket money. When he had cleared his feet, he went on his own once more and only occasionally had to come to my father for advice, as better times came along in the late 30s and during the Second War. He got married in the Second War and retired shortly after to Aberdeen.

Anybody who was taking a farm could rely on my father's help and shrewd advice, and many young men were extremely grateful for his guidance. Mrs Shepherd, the widow of a close friend, was left as tenant of a small farm that was providing a poor return to the lady. The trustees under the will were my father, Jim Durno of Upper Mill and James Keith of Pitmedden, all of whom agreed that my father, as a neighbour, could change the farm over to dairying and provide the widow with a reasonable living. The young solicitor opposed this, on the grounds that it meant borrowing money. He said that the will was so old that the named trustees no longer applied. He was opposing three of the toughest and most influential men in rural Aberdeenshire, who had no scruples about putting young and foolish men in their place. The dairying plan went ahead, prospered under my father's guidance and provided a far better living for Mrs Shepherd. At the same time he did not neglect his social duties. He played a big part in the build-up of the Scottish National Farmers Union, touring Scotland during his years in office. He became President in 1932 and during his time more than doubled the membership of the Union. He was paid the compliment of being asked to do another term, but refused on the grounds that his own business required his attention.

He was also a Governor of the North of Scotland College of Agriculture and was Chairman for many years. My uncle John had also been Chairman, some years previous to my father. At my parents' Golden Wedding celebration, an old friend who had been a senior official in the College told us that he was going through some woods in Morayshire with his Chairman, in this case Uncle John, and said, 'Lovely woods, Mr Mackie.' Uncle John replied, 'Aye, grand woods to walk in wi' a lass.' He appreciated this reply and many years later he was passing the same woods with his Chairman, Mr Maitland Mackie, and said, 'Lovely woods, Mr Mackie.' There was a pause, and then my father replied, 'Aye. I suppose these woods would be worth £1,000 an acre.'

In those days that community's centre was still the church. My father was a leading church elder in Tarves for fifty years and it was a central part of his life. For fifty years, he was Superintendent of the Sunday School. The general picture of Scottish Presbyterianism as a narrow, hard religion is not true of the Church of Scotland and was certainly not true of the ministers of Tarves Parish from 1930 onward. The Church of Scotland, as far as we were concerned, was a genuine liberal organisation, and for many years in my youth we had a minister, James Murray, who preached in a calm, ordinary voice, and was tolerant and indeed interested in divergent views. When I declined to join the Church at the usual age of 16, he said to my father he would far rather have someone who argued and thought about the situation than the many who passed through his Bible Classes with automatic acceptance.

One of the things my father did was to make money for the Church. He did not do this by ladling out money himself but by taking over the Glebe, about 10 acres of land. He farmed it very intensively during the good times and charged nothing for himself, while the tractor work was done at rates that made no loss to him, but were extremely cheap. He built up a fund big enough to refurbish the manse and this fund was also used for the raw materials of a Youth Hall. He then got the local tradesmen – the joiner, mason, slater and so on – to give their time free to direct the other volunteers dragged in by him. They built a very good Youth Hall extremely cheaply – and it stands there to this day.

Among other activities of the Parish was that relic of Victorian self-help, the Literary Society. My father was Secretary for many years until its demise and he played the main part in getting speakers to come to their monthly meetings. In 1940 he started writing a weekly bulletin of the family, the general farming activities and the College of Agriculture – the things he was doing and the happenings of the Parish. Every Sunday night he sat down with his book of thin paper with seven sheets of carbon and, using a ballpoint pen, pressed down through the news of the week. It was a mixture of serious news, farming news, family gatherings and downright mischief on occasion. He did this for over thirty years and it is a fascinating piece of social history. If you were in favour and had written, you might receive a top copy of the bulletin, but if you were out of favour, you got the bottom copy. I still have the originals: but a glossary is needed now of the people. I turn up a reference, for example, to Aggie and Mary – to me it at once recalls the Misses Simpson. They lived in the middle of The Square in Tarves and observed with keen interest everything that went on from behind beautifully laundered lace curtains.

There are many instances of my father's humanity. In Tarves we had an electrician and mechanic called Fred Middleton. He had six of a family. He was fond of a drop, but was an extremely clever man and mastered the mechanics of the motor car and the intricacies of the electrical system without formal training. Middleton once sent in a bill in which he grossly overstated his costs. I was grieve at North Ythsie at the time as a boy of 18, and as I had 5 per cent of the profits I obviously strove to keep the costs down. Full of fury, I said to my father that something must be done. He grinned and said, 'Middleton has a big family, and if you want to do something about it, you go and see him.' I went to see Middleton, pointed out the error of his ways and he looked at me, took the bill, amended it, and handed it back with these words: 'Geordie, your father is a gentleman. You are a young bugger.'

I remember too when one representative of a firm was found to be cheating on quite a significant scale. My father got hold of him and gave him a talking to and no doubt frightened him severely. Again, as a young pup, I said, 'Surely he should be prosecuted?' My father said, 'I know he has a young family, and prosecuting would do no good, whereas now he may have learned his lesson.'

The Parish of Tarves was once part of the estate of Haddo House, owned by the Marquis of Aberdeen who had an excellent reputation as an enlightened landlord. The international activities of the first Marquis were very expensive and large parts of the estate were sold off, mostly to the tenants. However, in the Tarves area, the Estate and the

Laird continued to play a big part in the life of the community. My father had a very good relationship with the Lord Aberdeen of the time, and indeed with his successor. My father built four new cottages on the farm after the First War and invited his landlord to see them when they were completed. After inspection, my father said, 'Now, Lord Aberdeen, we have a problem. I built the cottages, you supplied the wood and the Government gave us £100 towards each cottage. To whom do the cottages belong?' Lord Aberdeen's reply was, 'Well, in the first place we will cut out the Government!'

In Aberdeenshire there was a much better attitude towards landlords than I was later to find in Angus. There, the attitude was rather miserable – tenants sat on far better land at low rent and would not spend a penny on the landlord's property. My father was always conscious of the fact that it did not pay to be mean with a landlord when the rent was reasonable, and would always improve and maintain at his own expense when it was profitable to do so.

My mother was Mary Ann Yull, and she was a couple of years older than my father. They married in 1907 and there is a very sweet picture of their wedding at Little Ardo. She was the daughter of John Yull and had four brothers and a sister, all of whom emigrated. One or two of them died of taking too much drink. There was a great sadness about emigrating in the days before the First War; the likelihood of seeing sons and brothers again was really very small because of distance and expense. Among the few criticisms I would make of my father was that he might have taken my mother to Australia after the War to see her youngest brother, George, of whom she was very fond. She did see his son, John, but only when he came over to serve with the Royal Australian Air Force during the Second War. I suppose my father thought that he was always too busy to spare the time for the long sea journey, but she would have loved it.

My mother was extremely competent and the main thing I remember about my childhood was a feeling of total security and order. My mother, without doubt, regarded it as her duty to run the house and look after my father, while he provided the wherewithal, and she did this magnificently. Just after the war my mother did a broadcast about the farm kitchen, in which she described the life in her youth. I realise now the amount of hard work that she had to do running a big farmhouse in spite of having two maids and a nursemaid. She had three sons and three daughters. The single men also ate in the kitchen. While the maids milked the cows, she made the butter and also looked after the hens. My mother always liked to do the hens herself, and she kept for this purpose a hat in the back kitchen known as the Hen Hat, but for gardening she had a straw hat, kept at the front door, known as the Garden Hat. I cannot remember seeing much difference between the two hats, but there was a class distinction.

There is little doubt it was a hard life for all the women of the household. On washing days the maids had to rise at 3 o'clock in order to get the work done before milking the cows and attending to the men's breakfast. My grandfather was one of the last remaining people to kill a cattle beast and salt it away for the winter, and in this broadcast my mother described the process. It entailed the making of enormous numbers of sausages. Life eased a little when they had the house done up in about 1920 and modern fittings installed. By modern fittings I mean an enormous range. It required about 2 cwts of coal a day, humped from a cellar in order to feed the monster.

I may say that I did not really appreciate my mother until after the Second World War when I began to understand something of her humanity and indeed also to understand that she was, in some ways, wiser than my clever father. When I was farming in Angus, my parents were down on a visit to Benshie and a neighbour of mine, an ex RAF group captain, came to lunch. He was very entertaining and I think my mother appreciated him. A month or so later his wife left him, as he had made the nursemaid pregnant, and he was on his own. I was up at North Ythsie a couple of months after and my mother said to me, 'How is that nice man I met?' I told her the story and waited for the pursed lips and the strong disapproval. Instead of which she said, 'Oh what a pity! It used to happen a lot in the old days, especially when the wife was unwell. However, I do not think the sins of the flesh are as bad as the sins of the spirit, so I hope they will be all right.' It is to my great discredit that I was astonished by this. I should have realised that my mother had a warm heart, and also that she would not have been shocked. For the farming community in Aberdeenshire lived fairly close to nature.

CHAPTER 2

The Farm at North Ythsie

IT WAS IN THESE very secure Aberdeenshire surroundings that I grew up. When I was rising five I went to Tarves School. The class was divided into two: we had Higher Infants and Lower Infants, but all were under the care of the excellent Miss Thompson. There must have been at least forty of us all told. One keeper's son from Haddo House who came to start school was given a picture book to look at. He had never seen fanciful pictures before and suddenly burst into a roar of laughter and said, 'Look here – it's a lad on a duck's back!' This was considered most amusing by the sophisticated Higher Infants.

Miss Thompson was an admirable teacher and a very human person who never got the promotion she deserved. But I was subsequently ruled over by Miss Chalmers – a dragon of a woman – tall, good-looking, but with a fierce, narrow face. She had a reputation for improving the handwriting of her pupils but terrorised her classes. Happily for me, at the end of my first year, the school was overcrowded and this problem was solved by the Headmaster coming round and selecting a number of the brighter pupils for immediate promotion to the Qualifying Class under Miss Robertson, a bright, jolly woman. I enjoyed this, although I cannot say I worked very hard.

I enjoyed the dinners my sister Catherine and I used to get in the Aberdeen Arms in Tarves run by Mr and Mrs Tait – they had two very good looking daughters. I did the normal quantity of fighting. Then I went into Mr Pirie, the Headmaster's, class. This I greatly enjoyed. I used to make up historical charts and he talked to me a great deal and I think probably taught me more than I have learned at any similar period of my life. He realised that different children needed different treatment. The practical boys with no academic bent he introduced to gardening and taught them a great deal more about it than how to work a simple spade. He ruled the school with a very kindly hand. Nonetheless, of course, when particularly bad boys were sent to him from the other classes, he dealt out the usual amount of strapping. He lived to a great age and my brother Maitland took him up in an aeroplane when he was over 100.

I next proceeded for a couple of years to the Secondary School at Methlick, six miles away by bus or cycle. I think this was probably a mistake on my father's part, as one of the reasons for my two older brothers spending a period there was that they had an excellent Headmaster called Macdonald. By now he had been succeeded by a Mr Morrison, who although good, was not the same class of dominie. I went on to the Aberdeen Grammar School, where I had admirable lodgings in 50 Gladstone Place. I did two years there, taking my Highers when I was 15, and going on to university when I was newly 16 to do a B.Sc. in Agriculture.

I was a pushing young lout, who hated authority. I must say that life opened like a flower when I finished with school and the restrictions thereof. I should perhaps have gone into Sixth Year and had a year of enjoying English and History instead of going straight to university. My father also got me off doing a year's practical on a farm before going to university, and this, again, was perhaps a wrong move. But on consideration, it may be that he was wiser than I am now. My father may have thought, this is a thrusting sort of boy and the sooner we push him on to the next thing, the better for him.

My academic career did not prosper. I did not work at university. My father had been foolish enough to give me a motorcycle for passing University Entrance. Just at the time of my first exams, I ran into a motor car and was laid up with broken toes and other damages to my leg and head. This provided a good excuse, and although I passed Physics, Organic Chemistry with its enormous combination of Cs, Os and Hs seemed to me irrelevant, and I failed that exam twice. When I got to 17, I thought I could dispense with academic education and applied for a short service commission in the RAF. Needless to say, my father strongly disapproved. He pointed out that I would come out after four years with a few hundred pounds and no training to do anything except fly an aircraft. He also pointed out that if I ultimately wanted to be a farmer, having rejected taking an agricultural degree I would be extremely ill-equipped for it in any form. A little of this did sink home, but I persisted in my plan.

Then one day the grieve at North Ythsie came up to see my father and said he would have to leave at the Term – 28 May – because his wife was raising hell about some point or other. My father greeted this with the gravity it deserved, although it had happened before, and thought for a moment. Then he said, 'Well, Sandy. You have done well here, but I have sorted out this trouble two or three times before and I think that this time I will need to believe that you want to leave, and I will look for somebody else.'

As soon as news got out that he was leaving, a neighbouring farmer, Ernie Lee, was hot-foot over and Sandy was engaged to Boolroad within a week. I was witness to this and my father sat twiddling his watch chain for a few minutes. Then he said to this 17 year old young idiot, 'I will give you the grieve's job here at £50 a year and 5 per cent of the profits which, with your keep, is more than you are worth, but it will teach you about farming.'

To be grieve on a place with four pairs of horses tickled my vanity and I accepted. Thereupon the tension that had pervaded the house for the past few weeks disappeared. It was replaced perhaps by apprehension on my father's part as to how I could cope after the very experienced Sandy Milne.

Grieves were often men of great ability and force, fit easily to be Cabinet Ministers if their circumstances had been different. Sandy Milne was not clever like some of my father's grieves, but he was very conscientious and had the commanding presence necessary to lead the men on the farm. He was, like so many others, an ex-soldier. The very acute old cattleman, Geordie More, who had been fee'd (engaged) on the neighbouring place to Sandy Milne during the War, said to me once with a twinkle in his eye, 'Sandy Milne was an affa bonny whistler when he was at the ploo, but the day his papers came to join the army, there wis nae whistling that day.'

Sandy Milne maintained afterwards, however, that he had enjoyed the War. It is said, with what truth I don't know, that when he had his teeth out, he turned up next day with a gleaming set of new teeth in which large chunks of gold were flashing. Somebody said, 'Sandy, where did you get those teeth?' His reply was, 'I took them aff a deid German officer.'

Sandy was a tremendous man to work. In those times he had to turn the potato sorter or riddle by hand, and as he did this for most of the winter days, his right arm was very strong indeed. He would march into the stables five minutes before yoking time and stand passing the time of day. At about two minutes before yoking time, he would walk down the stable: 'Foreman to the plough; second man to the plough;

third and fourth man to driving turnips; fifth man to driving turnips.'
At precisely a quarter past six in the morning, the foreman's first horse
would be going out the door of the stable.

Sandy was not a very neat builder of ricks, but he did what my father
always insisted was the essence of stack building, and that is to keep up
the heart of the stack, so that the outside sheaves could not help sloping
down and therefore ran the water properly, whether the stack was
thatched or not. Another one of his great assets was that he could start
at the first kick the awful oil engine that drove the mill, whereas I often
had to fight for half an hour to get the bloody thing going. He was, in
short, a typical example of a top grieve of those days.

And this was the man I had to follow. The news that I was to be
grieve was meant to be secret, but it quickly got out amongst the men
and, while riding in a cart with the foreman, I realised there was no
point when he said to me, 'Aye Geordie. I hear you are tae get your
name up aboot this place.' On 29 May 1937 I therefore strode into the
stable and braved the grins of the men who were awaiting my bungled
first orders. I threw the line in the time-honoured manner, giving each
his instructions, and off they went, singling turnips. I must say I left
them alone the first day while I went about preparing other jobs. When
I did join the turnip singlers, I had a devil of a job to keep up: the
foreman had obviously said to himself, 'We will teach young Geordie a
lesson,' and went at a good deal beyond his normal speed.

The object was two-fold. First and foremost was to single the turnips
so that a space of about 10 inches would be left between them, allowing
them to develop to a decent size. The next and equally important task
was to clean off the weeds by pushing them into the centre of the drill,
where they could be killed with a horse hoe until such time as the
turnips grew and the space was covered by the shaws, thereby keeping
the weeds down.

At North Ythsie we had an implement called a scarifier which pared
both sides of the drills taking away many, but not all, of the weeds. The
great art of hoeing was to leave only one seedling turnip. In my drill,
because of the foreman's speed, there were many doubles. Happily, the
foreman tired of his excessive speed after a while and thought that he
had done enough to teach the young grieve a lesson, while I grew more
expert at singling and less ashamed of my drill.

The men were really extraordinarily good about it and never tried to
take advantage of me unless I got above myself. When the dung was

being driven out from the midden to the fields, the practice was that the first horseman's pair of carts were first in the midden and the other men had little jobs to do until their turn came. The carts were filled by hand, the horseman filling his first cart and the grieve filling the second cart. The foreman was called Bisset, a good horseman with whom I got on well. Being a healthy young brute, I tore into the filling of the second cart then walked over to Bisset and said, 'I'll give you a hand.' He flushed with anger and for the rest of the day went at a pace which took a whole lot of fire out of the belly of the young grieve, because whereas he had to fill a cart once every forty minutes or so, I had to fill four carts to his one and he set the pace. By nightfall, we had driven out more dung in a day than we had driven out before, and there was a very tired, but very much wiser, young grieve.

Spring and summer were busy periods. It was absolutely essential to get the grain in early because it had been clearly shown by Mr Findlay of the North of Scotland College that, on average, every day you delayed after 14 April in the sowing of oats cost a bushel of yield, so that a week's delay would cost a quarter of oats which, at £1 a quarter over 200 acres, was £200. In those days, that might well have been the difference between profit and loss. All the work at this time was, of course, done by horses and the sowing was done by the grieve with a broadcast sower, later superseded by the drill on most farms. The grieve's skill consisted in working out the placement of the sacks of seed grain, so that he could gauge exactly how the seed rate was running as he crossed the field and came to the set out sacks, adjusting the machine as he went.

Potato planting came next and, lastly, turnips were sown. This was closely followed by the making of hay and the run up to harvest. In late autumn, after the first thresh, oats were driven to the miller at the other side of Tarves three miles away. I remember three pairs of carts setting off with the oats. As seven cottages and the farmhouse had to be supplied with about ten hundredweights each it must have required about six tons of oats. Some weeks later, the carts went back for the oatmeal and it was distributed round the cottages and the farmhouse. The meal girnal was a box about five feet high and four feet by six feet. It was the store for the oatmeal for at least a year. When the big girnal on the back porch was being filled, the oatmeal had to be tramped down. As a young boy this had been my job – one of the sacks was turned outside in, I was inserted and tramped in the bags as they were emptied. Meal was the foundation of the diet and, well tramped in a girnal, would keep for years.

Because most farms were too busy getting the oats into the stack yard and off the ground to do any threshing, the millers often had a shortage at harvest. So there was a premium for oats at harvest time. A few farmers, including my father, used to take advantage of this by threshing out of the stook. At North Ythsie we would thresh out at least a 40-acre field. This was a very useful practice: apart from getting a better price, you also got a bigger yield as the oats contained a rather higher percentage of moisture and there was no waste in double handling. In order to do this, one had to scour the country for extra men and, with the use of my mother's car, I was reasonably successful in doing so.

On one occasion I assembled a squad of tinkers and got a good deal of threshing done the first week. I paid them in the back kitchen and had to go for more money, leaving the wages sheet on top of the oatmeal girnal. When I came back, there was uproar. The tinkers had read the wages sheet with their descriptions, which were as follows: 'The fat tink', 'the insured tink' and 'the scabby tink'. They resented it deeply. One said, 'I'm no tink. My father has property in Pitmedden.' The scabby tink was particularly indignant, and they went off swearing they would never ever work for me again.

There was a great, old-fashioned satisfaction about harvest. I was young and very fit and rather gloried in the work. My stacks were not very neat, but they got better, and we cleared out fields for threshing at high speed. We built the straw into long ricks which we called soos, as I suppose the shape was that of a long pig. When harvest was over and the sheaves built in the cornyard, this was called 'getting winter'.

The cutting and stooking was again an art in itself. Many of the fields at North Ythsie were on quite steep slopes, so for three horses to pull the heavy binder up the hill was far too laborious. One had to cut a diagonal strip across and cut the field sections to enable the horses to keep up the necessary speed to work the binder. When you finished cutting with the binders it was called 'clyack'. The stooks had to be lined up with the prevailing wind, so that the wind blew down the centre of the stook or north and south and both sides got some sun.

The worst job of the whole lot was setting up or restooking in a bad harvest. It was both uncomfortable and disheartening. When 'clyack' was achieved, the leading in started, and my father was particularly insistent that you did not wait until the whole stook was dry. Very often five sheaves out of a stook of ten sheaves would be dry, while the five on the other side away from the wind were wet, so that he would insist on the grieve going to check the number of dry sheaves and getting a start immediately, leaving the wet sheaves to be re-stooked.

Neither of the harvests at North Ythsie during my time as grieve were bad, so that I did not experience a really nasty harvest until farming on my own after the War. When the fields were cleared, the stacks had then to be thatched. Very little wheat was grown in Aberdeenshire at that time, so oat straw was drawn out to make the thatching material and then put on the stacks and roped down with sparta ropes. Walking round the cornyard, it was necessary to look where you put your feet as there was no outside loo on the farm. But I must say that at the end of my first harvest, with everything thatched, I felt very pleased with myself. It gave me a good feeling to walk round, count the 'rucks', and admire my handiwork.

After the potatoes were lifted and pitted, we went into the routine of winter. This consisted really of seeing that the beasts were fed and as much as possible was ploughed for the following spring, leaving the lea ground to the last, because it could be ploughed when other land was too wet and also so that the stock, particularly sheep, could be grazed there for as long as possible.

The basis of winter feeding, and indeed of winter work, was the turnip, which many generations of farm workers curse. They were topped and tailed (with a tapner, which was a small machete with a hook on the end), or simply tailed if the shaws were still fresh, then put into rows, loaded into the carts by hand, driven home to the turnip shed and stacked up there.

The weather played an enormous part in our lives and there were many, many 'bad day' jobs to be done, maintenance of all sorts – making ropes and cleaning up – while horsemen took care of their harness. In my first winter as grieve, we got warning on the weather forecast of a great storm and my father said, 'You must fill the neep sheds.' So all hands were put to the task and the turnip sheds were filled to overflowing. A storm did come, and our turnips lasted until we could get at fresh ones. The cattle were tied by the neck and the cattleman fed them turnips and straw – seldom, if ever hay – and a little dry feed, but a skilful cattleman could fatten cattle on turnips and straw, with very little extra linseed cake or oats.

The cattle byres were warm and friendly places. The double rows of cattle, newly strawed and lying chewing the cud contentedly, were pleasing to the eye of the farmer and made nonsense of any claim that it was cruel to tether cattle by the neck. Cattleman Geordie More counted all his steps, so always finished his cattle before a younger cattleman, because he had everything worked out, including the number of turnips that each stall would eat. When finished, he used to go home whether it was stopping time or not, and he was such a good cattleman that nobody queried this practice.

Although big changes were on the way, the organisation of an Aberdeenshire farm had not really changed in the century up to 1936. The horse was the power unit, organised in pairs. On North Ythsie at that time we had four pairs of horses, for a farm of between 300 and 400 acres. Two of the horsemen were married, with a tied house, and two were single men who slept in the chaumer (or bothy).

There were two married cattlemen, who had a byre and 40 cattle each, chained by the neck. In addition, there was an orraman, who was much more skilled than his title implies. 'Orra' can mean untidy, but an orraman was a man who was not dedicated to one type of work, unlike a cattleman. He had to be able to turn his hand to everything. Another man was a gardener/orraman whose main priority was the farm, not the garden – to my mother's disgust.

In the house at North Ythsie, besides my father, mother and six of a family, there were two maids and a nursemaid or mother's help. We had seven cottages and the chaumer. Cottar houses were nearly always in pairs, which encouraged both social intercourse and, occasionally, strife. The chaumer was a social centre for single and married men and young boys. Mothers would certainly not let their daughters go near there. Right opposite was South Ythsie with four cottages and another chaumer so we had a community altogether of some seventy souls – men, women and children.

The farm servants of the north east of Scotland were men of independence. They lived tough lives, but they had a great pride in their craft. They made a bargain for a year if married, six months if single, and they fulfilled their side of the bargain, looked after their horses, worked long hours and took a pride in their work. Woe betide any farmer who didn't keep his side of the bargain, and bad farmers didn't get the good men. It was understood that if a man fell ill, the farmer took his National Insurance money. His pay and, more important, the perquisites continued as usual. These consisted of half a gallon of fresh milk a day, six bolls of oatmeal a year, one ton of coal, one ton of potatoes and keep for twelve hens plus a free house (not always a very good one). If a man had an able wife in good health, then they could live a hard but full life. But if the wife was not an able organiser or was in bad health, then real poverty would strike the family.

We had an extraordinary example of the length a man would go to retain his independence. On North Ythsie, Malcolm was an excellent horseman and a good foreman. He had been with us three years. As was the custom, I went to him in February to ask him to stay another year and make a bargain for the year. He replied that he was going to have a shift. I offered more money, up from £60 a year to £65, but he was adamant. I reported this to my father and asked him to see Malcolm, in case his pride had been hurt by not being asked personally by the boss.

My father was a highly skilled handler of men and, when he saw Malcolm, the first thing he asked was if he was displeased with his pair of horses. Malcolm, with a touch of heat, replied that they were a grand pair when he got them and even better now. The old man then went on to ask if the wife was pleased with the house. Malcolm replied that the wife liked the house. My father then came to the third important factor, 'What about the sillar?' 'The sillar's as good as I'd get fae ony hungry fermer.' The old man in exasperation then could only say, 'Why the devil are you leaving then?' Malcolm came to the sad but proud point. 'I'm leaving because I'm getting to like the place, and if ye like a place ower much, the fermer has a hold on ye.' At that my father knew he was beaten, and wished him luck.

CHAPTER 3

An Aberdeenshire Boyhood

OUR WHOLE FAMILY had a great tour in 1927. With the exception of my young sister, Catherine, who at that time was only four, we set off in my father's car, a Minerva, an enormous brute of a thing. It was very up to date in that the self-starter was on the key. My mother sat in the front with my father. The three eldest of the family – John, Jean and Mike – sat in the back seat. There was plenty of room and a large square picnic basket with a rug over it was placed in front of them. On this I sat, with my sister Mary. The bell tents used by the shepherds for lambing came with us: they were folded inside two large sacks labelled 'Scotch Seed Oats' which were placed in the wings of the car alongside the bonnet and behind the mudguard. On the back was a pile of other luggage and more cases. In this way, we left for Edinburgh.

We camped in a very nice site by the sea belonging to a friend of my father's, Jack Dale. We pitched the tents and the whole family went into Edinburgh to the theatre. The elder members went to see a Shaw play, but my brother John took Mary and me, aged twelve and eight, to see a drama entitled 'Rob Roy'. I did not like the shooting. My poor brother was also extremely embarrassed by his sister Mary. During the interval she went off to the lavatory. By this time people were returning to their seats and, half way along, she turned and said in an enormous whisper to John, 'Do I need a penny?' She came all the way back for it, to the grins of the numbers round about and to the great embarrassment of the young man of 18.

From Edinburgh we drove on to Yorkshire. We looked at two or three farms my father was interested in, and came home to Aberdeenshire in triumph, with the bags still showing 'Scotch Seed Oats' and the family in high good humour, having got used to sleeping on the hard ground.

As a boy and then as a young man, my social life usually revolved about the farm at North Ythsie and the village. Tarves was about two miles from the farm and vans came round supplying groceries and butcher meat (not often bought by the cottars). Fishwives came with fish and travelling packmen displayed their wares to anyone who could afford to buy. In Tarves itself, with a population of some 300 souls, the main shops were round the square. Beside the War Memorial we had the watchmaker; round the corner we had the Post Office run by the Hendry family. Next door we had the shoemaker, Mr Gibb, a big shop employing six or seven people repairing shoes – it was an old family business. Across the way, on the south side, we had the tailor, Mr McHattie. He was an enthusiastic photographer and had the first ciné camera in the district with which he took pictures of local events and showed them round the county at the WRI (including our wedding in 1944).

On the same side was the Aberdeen Arms Hotel run by Mr and Mrs Tait, where I had my school dinners as an infant. Next door to that there were two houses, one occupied by Miss Chalmers, the fearsome school teacher, and the other was Duthie's, the general merchants, selling everything from sewing needles to grass seed. Duthie's employed quite a few people and was the great centre of the village. The North of Scotland Bank was next door, run by Mr Duthie Webster, the rich man of the village. Next door to that we had Tarves Public School, and then across the road, William Cumming, the baker, famous for his hard biscuits which were sold all over Aberdeenshire. He had prospered greatly and built a fine house.

Moving up the street back towards the Square, we had the saddler, a very nice man with a limp, whose shop was a sub-centre for gossip. Next came George Presley, the butcher, one of the characters of the area. He had been awarded the Military Medal in the First War. Next to him was the joiner, William Massie – an enterprising man, expanding his business – who built a lot of big sheds for my father. Next was Bob Reid, the blacksmith – a great favourite of mine, particularly on bad days when I could make an errand up and stand by the fire chatting. Beside the smiddy was the Melvin Hall where great events took place. Round the corner from the police station, going up the hill towards the 'pleasure park', we had Middleton, the motor engineer and electrician. The doctor's house and surgery was across the road and the schoolmaster's house was at the bottom of the Square. On the Aberdeen road, just on the edge, we had the church, the graveyard and the manse. Although perhaps it was already being eroded by the introduction of Kerr's bus service to Aberdeen at frequent intervals, Tarves was a complete community.

With a penny line and a penny hook bought from Duthie's, I used to go fishing on the farm itself. The Sonah burn ran right by us for about a couple of miles. My rod was a rowan stick got from the bushes and trimmed to the right length. There was no question of fishing with flies – the worm was the bait. Sometimes we set a line, but invariably ended up with an eel – which we did not appreciate. There was a considerable degree of skill in dropping the worm quietly into a rougher bit of water and letting it float into the pool, and quite often I would catch two or three fish. The burn had some nice brown trout that varied from a third to two thirds of a pound. I will never forget one magic day when the trout went mad and took the bait immediately. That afternoon I caught thirteen.

When I was nine years old the second horseman at North Ythsie was a very able young man called James Low. He was always pushing the foreman, who was a good man but not as able as James Low. We boys had heard some of the horsemen's secrets: one was that the horse hates anything to do with the pig and especially, of course, pig shit. While the men were at their dinner, I got hold of some pig shit and rubbed it inside the collar of James Low's first horse. When the foreman got up at one minute to one to harness, James Low, as usual, was out of his seat like a shot – on one arm he had the saddle, which he threw on the back, with the other he took the collar off its hook and was up in front of his first horse in, I suppose, about five seconds. To his astonishment the horse jibbed, it jibbed again and again. He looked at the collar and saw me standing in the doorway. He grabbed his whip and came after me. Happily, he had on his tackety boots and I was quite fleet in those days, and after three fields he returned home to clean his collar and yoke his pair. I may say that we became firm friends in later years.

We played all the usual games around the farm, building little houses between the ricks, where we had picnics until they were found and destroyed by an irate grieve. We rode on the empty carts and enjoyed taking the horses out to the horse field in the summer. That allowed the horsemen to go straight home after their nine and a half hour day, plus stable time.

On top of the hill there stands a monument to the Premier Earl of Aberdeen, about 80 feet high with a spiral staircase up to the top. There was a magnificent view across to the hills, with Bennachie standing out, and back over to the Buchan plain. We used to run races round the parapet. No one ever fell off, but our parents must on occasions have been extremely anxious.

Every Thursday my father put the bull calves (the females were reared for replacement cows) from the dairy farm at Thomaston into a big box he had on the back of the Minerva and he drove them 20 miles down to North Ythsie, selling them to people on the way. On one occasion he remembered a small crofter up a rather bad road, who had bought a calf from him some years before. He went up and saw the crofter, who greeted him in a kindly manner and said, 'Ah, you have come to see the calf,' and led the way into the byre where an enormous brute of four or five years old was eating his head off. My father was astonished and said surely it was time he was sold, to which the crofter replied, 'Ah well. The wife liked the calfie, so we just kept it.'

Although it was illegal, I learned to drive when I was about 12 and sometimes in the early morning I would deliver the calves which my father had brought down from Thomaston. Once, he had promised a small farmer called Geordie Hay a calf, and said it would cost him £3 or thereby. This was a particularly good calf, so he said to me to try to get £3.10s. I wondered why he smiled as he said so. I think I must have been 13 or 14 at the time and I set off with the calf early one morning and drove the two miles to East Shethin. Geordie Hay looked at the calf, said it was a good calf and said, 'Now your father said £3.' I said, 'Na, na. This is a better calf – a £3.10s. calf.' After a great deal of argument I threatened to take the calf home, and he paid the £3.10s. When he saw my father in church the next Sunday he said, 'Maitland, you can die when you like. That young devil can live without you!' I think he thought I was going to keep the 10 shillings for myself.

After seven years on the farm, the huge Minerva for which my father had paid over £700 got a little weary and he sold it. To his disgust, he only received £100. He then swore he would not buy a new car and instead purchased a second-hand Straight 8 Wolseley which had been beautifully maintained and chauffeur driven. I think it was only two or three years old and he paid about £300 for it. It was an admirable car.

We had a grass tennis court on the lawn in front of the house. It was very difficult to keep, and plans were made for a hard blaize court behind the house. But the work proceeded only when the farm staff were available in a slack time to drive stones to level up the chosen piece of land. It took about five years before the great day arrived when the court was ready for play: I used to play after work in the summer and thought nothing about it, although the working day at that time was a full nine hours (and a half day on Saturday).

When I became grieve, I played rugby for Aberdeenshire, having previously played for the University. Aberdeenshire was a very amiable Club and had been going for some eighty years. It was captained by a friend, George Raeburn, an apprentice solicitor in Aberdeen, in a firm in which the senior partner was his uncle, James Hay. We played energetically and drank too much of a Saturday.

I went to a Conservative Party dance at Fyvie Castle with a friend, Max Scott. As soon as I got into the marquee I spotted a crowd which contained a very good looking girl. I immediately asked her to dance. This was Lindsay Sharp, who was to become my wife. She and a party of school friends were camping at Methlick on the Braes of Gight, which they did quite safely and happily in those times. The whole bunch of the girls came to North Ythsie to have baths, but apart from that they managed perfectly well. This was in the summer of 1938 and Lindsay and I saw each other constantly after that. I got to know her formidable mother. Lindsay was the youngest of the family and, as often happens, the busy mother depended a lot on the youngest daughter. We met often in Aberdeen, using my mother's Morris 8 and sometimes my father's car.

The church, of course, played a big part in our lives on Sunday. We went to Sunday School and then stayed on for church, my father being superintendent of the Sunday School. I became for a time a Sunday School teacher, on my father's insistence, but the parents of my class complained to the minister that, although their children looked forward greatly to Sunday School, they were not being taught anything about Christianity. Instead they were told serial adventure stories made up by George Mackie. I enjoyed inventing these tales and the class enjoyed them too, but my services were dispensed with.

After church in the morning Sundays were quite relaxed. When we got back, my father and whichever sons were at home would go round the cattle, inspecting each one in the byre to see if any were fat and ready to go. This was followed by Sunday dinner – always a sirloin roast and apple duff or trifle. The young were then released on to the farm while my parents, I dare say, had a snooze. I taught myself to shoot (not very well) with the old farm gun, but on this farm, as my father was a tenant, we only shot rabbits and hares. My brother had an occasional shoot on Westerton and Easterton and I used to sometimes go over to Little Ardo, which was owned by my father, where on one occasion I had a right and a left at snipe, which I have never done since.

When my father went to North Ythsie he had no need for a grieve, as being a keen young man, he did the grieve's job himself. The admirable grieve on North Ythsie had been William Cumming and he had to leave, but, as I understand it, was immediately re-employed by my grandfather as a shepherd and no doubt in other jobs. Willie Cumming was the perfect example of an able young farm servant who with different chances would have made a far better Cabinet Minister than many we know of. He told tales of his early life in the bothy. Sometimes, he said, it was so cold that he took his boots to bed with him so that they would not be frozen in the morning.

When he took his first out-farm of Westerton, Rothienorman, my father immediately engaged Willie Cumming as grieve and he thereafter put him in charge of other farms in that area, so that Willie Cumming was eventually managing four farms, Westerton, Easterton, Thomaston and Denend. He managed them with great attention and ability for many years and married his second wife from the area, and was altogether a figure in the agricultural world. At that time my father was doing experiments with artificial manure on grassland for ICI and Willie Cumming handled both the experiments and the visitors with great skill. He and my father used to discuss the moves for the next week every Thursday, so that not an hour of any man was wasted. It was a very happy relationship; we children sometimes went up to spend part of our holidays at Westerton with the Cummings.

Willie Cumming had a very soft attractive voice and the Doric sounded musical when spoken by him – which is not universal. On one occasion Colonel Pollit, a director of ICI, who was conducting the grassland experiments on my father's farm, came up in the late autumn to have a look, and he asked Willie Cumming about the tufts of grass and why they were not cut down to let fresh grass come up. Willie Cumming's reply was, 'Ah weel, you see, when it comes sna, the wee ewes can scrape with their feeties when they see the tuft and get tae the grass.' In another field Pollit again said, 'Mr Cumming, tell me again about the tufts of grass.' Willie Cumming replied, 'Well, ye see, in time of sna the sheepies can scrape where they see a tuftie and get some feed, but if it is bare, they widnae ken where tae scrape.' The manager of SAI, Aberdeen, leaned over his boss and whispered, 'I can explain this to you later.' Pollit turned to him and snapped, 'Shut up man! Of course I understand. I just wanted to hear him say it again.'

When my brother Maitland was getting married, it was fairly obvious to Willie Cumming, who by this time was approaching retiring age, that one of the farm houses would be required for Maitland, and furthermore that Maitland was of an age to take over the management of Westerton and Easterton. So he decided to retire and bought a bungalow near Oldmeldrum. This greatly pleased his wife as she would have a house near her relations. Willie Cumming then informed my father of his plans. My father, who was grateful for his consideration, disliked the plan. He thought Willie Cumming, whom he regarded as being at the height of his powers, should not retire to a bungalow beside Oldmeldrum.

My father had a cousin who had a small estate beside Newburgh with a good farm called Drums. John Smith was retiring from farming and moving to Newburgh House. My father saw his cousin and got him to promise to rent the farm to Willie Cumming. He, of course, jumped at the chance, but his wife was furious and would not speak to my father. Some people might consider it a little high-handed of my father, but he knew his man and Willie Cumming would have wilted away in a bungalow beside Oldmeldrum. They moved into the farm. It had a very nice house, and prospered greatly. Two years later Mrs Cumming apologised to my father, and said that he was right. He lived there, farming happily, for many years and bought the farm from the landlord. So in his lifetime he went from taking his boots to bed to make them wearable in the frosty mornings to being laird of a very good farm.

In my Easter holidays from school, I used to be a lot with our shepherd at North Ythsie, Cabie Campbell. He was a good shepherd and a pretty cunning chap, who did not believe in the system then in vogue of penning up lambing ewes individually. He fenced off a portion of the field; ewes close to lambing were brought in there and a few shelter fences were put up, but otherwise the sheep moved about as normal. He got as good results or better than the more painstaking method of fencing the ewes. He slept in a movable hut which had replaced the bell tents the shepherds used to use at lambing.

He always had a bottle of whisky to give a teaspoonful to any lamb that needed reviving. But when I was lambing with him I noticed that the lambs in fact got a spoon of hot, sweet tea, which he said was far better for them. It was the shepherd needed the whisky. He said, 'Dinna tell your auld man.' Years afterwards, my father told me that he knew perfectly well that the whisky was for the shepherd, but thought that he deserved it, being out in all weathers and at all times.

For many years there had been a Horse Fair at Aikey Brae on a Saturday and on the Sunday there was a tremendous gathering of people out to enjoy themselves. This was disapproved of strongly by the more sober and responsible of the elders in Aberdeenshire. When I was about 14 my parents went on holiday, and Cabie Campbell the shepherd and I went to Aikey Brae on the Sunday. It was a great treat, and I thoroughly enjoyed it and trusted the discretion of the shepherd. My elder brother, Maitland, disapproved. He gave the show away deliberately at Sunday dinner by saying did I enjoy Aikey Brae with the shepherd? My parents were reasonably shocked. I was mortified, furious, and attacked my brother that afternoon and had to be pulled off him as he was turning black from the pressure of my hands round his neck. Brotherly love was soon resumed.

I had a collie pup called Moses which I gave to Cabie Campbell to train. I was at the back of the hill one day in a thick fog, when out of the mist a great voice spoke: 'Moses, you bugger, come here!' That was Cabie. Cabie Campbell also taught me how to clip and to clip fast. When I later went down to Norfolk in 1939, I was astonished to see the men first of all – two of them – catch the sheep, tie up its feet, then put it on a sort of grid and clip, whereupon I showed them that you grab the ewe, put it on its side, turn it over, and thus speed up the process enormously. Unfortunately, in so doing, I nicked the skin on one or two ewes and when I looked at my clipping, quite apart from the odd bits of blood, their shearing was much closer and I realised the difficulty of changing the method.

Because the land was hard and at a higher latitude, the Aberdeenshire farmers always had to work harder than those in the counties of England. Although some farms were given up by tenants who could not make a living, they were taken over by people like Sandy Wishart. He was able to make a profit where others had failed. His type of farming was not particularly desirable, but at least it kept the land in shape. He followed the rotation, cut labour to the minimum and bought in bulk. He never gathered weeds by hand but ploughed them down. One of his sayings was, 'Weeds belong to the Laird.'

In Aberdeenshire any new idea was taken up with great vigour. Lawson's, the bacon curers, moved from Fife to Dyce in Aberdeenshire, where a co-operative effort at bacon curing had failed, and took over the factory. Frank Lawson asked my father to become a Director and to put in some money. The object was to encourage other farmers to follow my father's example and start producing pigs on contract for the factory. The whole idea took off and a lot of farmers took up both pig feeding and breeding. Lawsons prospered and did extremely well. Eventually, unfortunately, they sold out to Unilever who abandoned the factory after a few years. If the Lawson family had still been in control, they would, without doubt, have fought through the difficult times. This is the danger of the large company who, when they get into difficulties, get rid of the outlying factories.

The hen was taken up with some enthusiasm on a commercial scale by a number of people, although in the main it remained the preserve of the farmer's wife and the eggs were marketed through the travelling grocer. Like everything else, breeding became more scientific and eventually reached the peak of efficiency in the battery hen. Happily it is now returning to more humane methods.

Dairying was very much in the doldrums until the farmers of Aberdeenshire got together to form the Aberdeen Milk Agency – able to market the milk properly, instead of piecemeal amongst a number of dairy retailers, who took maximum advantage of the unorganised producers. The Milk Marketing Board Act of 1933 made a terrific difference. It encouraged farmers all over the country to go into milk, instead of concentrating around Aberdeen and the other towns in the area. It used its monopoly wisely and spread the transport costs.

Travelling through Aberdeenshire at that time, the steadings and the houses did not look particularly good. But they were at least kept wind and watertight; the land was never let out of shape and when the 1939/45 War happened a great increase in production took place. My father was on the Executive Committee, the wartime body which controlled and encouraged farming production in the area and had responsibility for getting farmers to plough up old grassland and grow more cereals.

When I was home on leave I spent a day going round some of these small farms with him. The method was simple. My father, who certainly knew nearly every one of them, opened his remarks by saying, 'Now, you will need to grow more oats for the war effort.' The reply was invariably, 'Maitland, I would never be able to hairst it.' Whereupon my father would take out an old envelope and explain that the Executive Committee would help with the cutting and then, more importantly, he would explain how much money they could reckon to get off ploughing up say an extra ten acre field. This was the clinching argument. On all the farms we visited that day, it never failed.

The War did one very good thing; it stopped the practice of married men engaging for only a year. Single men only engaged for six months from the May Term (28 May), and the November Term (28 November). But married men were asked to stay in late February or March. If not asked they moved at the May Term. Every year a decision had to be taken one way or another, leading to a feeling of impermanence, which was not helpful. When the War ended that was not to return. This is not to say that moves did not take place, but no longer was there the invitation every year, to move or not.

After the war too, the houses were to become better looked after; they were improved in order to keep the good men and the gardens became a source of pride and enjoyment, instead of merely a vehicle in which to grow kale and potatoes. Things improved greatly in the countryside and I think that my father's remark, made humorously, was nevertheless a true one when he said, 'The men are doing much better – I see pyjamas on the line.' Although wages and conditions for farm workers are now much improved, mechanisation has removed their numbers. With their decline has gone the whole way of life I knew in Aberdeenshire as a young man.

CHAPTER 4

In England, 1939

'I AM GOING TO New Zealand to have a look at that fine country,' I said to my father. After two years at North Ythsie, during which I suppose I had turned into a moderately competent grieve and got a good deal of experience of stock, both dairying and pig farming, I had again got itchy feet. My father considered this, and said to me, 'You are not yet fully trained, although you think you are. To give you experience, why don't you see my friend, Major Keith, and see if he would give you a job with his farming company?'

The Weasingham Farming Company was by that time running to about 5,000 acres in Norfolk. The Company had been started by Jim Keith and his cousin Alec, both of whom had farms in the county and who saw the opportunities of a great deal of land going derelict, which could be farmed by able men like themselves on a new system. They took on as Partner and Managing Director a very effective young Dane called Brun, and by this time they were very much in his hands.

I thought Norfolk was a good idea. But Major Keith said to me, 'Well, it is very difficult for me to give you a job short term as a bailiff, because obviously we want people to stay for some time, but let me think about it. I will consult your father.' Whereupon the two old devils put their heads together, and evolved a scheme. I realised, of course, that I was again being manoeuvred, but by this time there was nothing I could do about it. As the company was expanding, they needed junior managers and Major Keith offered me the job of stock manager. As I have since gathered, he and my father had decided that when I was 21 and was due to get the stocking of a 300 acre farm from my father, I could make up my mind whether to stay or go on my own. I went down to Norfolk to look round, accepted the job and started at the end of February 1939.

I was delighted to find that the Norfolk men touched their caps and called me Sir. Father's men had called me 'Geordie', and I thought this a great improvement. But I soon discovered the dairy herds were appallingly badly managed. On the first morning I went up to one farm, High House, at 4 o'clock, which was when they were supposed to start milking, to find nobody about. I kicked at a few doors and the head cowman came out and said he had slept in, most unfortunately, got the other men out, and milking started. I read them a lecture about being on time and departed after the morning's work was finished. I came back in the evening and all was spruce and up to time.

The next morning I went to the second farm, Palgrave Hall, and exactly the same performance was found there, with men late. The place was dirty and slackness was very evident. I read the same lecture there and stayed for the morning and in the afternoon went to Weasingham Main Farm, where there was a Scots dairy cattleman. There I saw a rather different story: not perhaps as clean as it should have been, but the cows were looked after and milked on time and the milking records showed that this was a good cattleman. His name was Wallace. This was the farm that Brun stayed on and although a number of things needed tightening up, the dairy herd there was doing reasonably well.

The next morning I went to the fourth dairy farm and found them up and doing at the correct time – the word had obviously got about. By this time I had a fair idea that these men were not like our Aberdeenshire men. The next day, instead of going to the fifth farm, I went to the first farm. I found them in bed, expecting me on the fifth farm. By this time I kicked up one helluva row and spoke to them about completion of their contract.

I had a lot of work to do in weeding out bad cows, attacking mastitis, and so on. It was a very interesting and constructive period for me because I saw an entirely new set-up. I found that the men, if properly looked after, were not as bad as all that, and we did improve the performance of the dairy herds by quite a lot. Brun, however, didn't like me. He was unpleasant, but as I had direct access to Captain Alec Keith, I was not particularly bothered by his hostility.

I had a salary of £5 a week, the use of an old Austin 12 Touring Model (which would be worth a fortune if I had it today) and I shared a house, as lodger, with another young manager, a Dane called Oleson who managed and was a partner in the West Lexham Farming Company, another of the Keiths' companies. West Lexham was a smaller company, but Oleson was an extremely able young man and was making a good job of it.

I paid 35s. a week as my share of the expenses and we were fed and watered by the pigman's wife, Mrs Field. We had our simple meals in a vast dining room in which there was a table and four chairs. Mrs Field had the idea that farmers should eat meat, and we were served rather primitively cooked meat at practically every meal. Eventually we rebelled and said we wanted a meal solely of vegetables. She placed the platter of vegetables on the table and ran from the room, crying at the shame of it all.

We fed and lived in a fairly basic way until Oleson's mother came over from Denmark to visit her son. I think that she was quite horrified at what she found, for a great revolution took place. All sorts of things – furniture, napkins, tablecloths – were bought, to Oleson's financial disadvantage, and she proceeded to cook proper, wonderful, Danish meals. She was joined after a week by some more relations from Denmark, whereupon we had absolutely superb food in vast quantity and I was introduced to the salute 'Skol' whenever you took a drink. After about three weeks, however, she went home and we returned to our modest standard of living.

Apart from having read *England, Their England* by A.G.M. Macdonell, I had really little knowledge of English life, and approached it with enthusiasm. I went to the local church at Lexham, a very pretty building, on my first Sunday there, and was rather bemused by what appeared to me to be a High Church service. The responses and the kneeling I viewed with disapproval, but I rather enjoyed the shortness of the sermon and the attractive church. The vicar was a kind man with a couple of daughters a bit older than me, and he asked me along for tea and tennis.

I was tickled to find him exactly as such men were portrayed in books. He had been to Cambridge and he had rowed for his College; a pair of oars were crossed on the wall in the hall. I think he was probably amused too by this large, raw young man out of Aberdeenshire, but certainly the whole family was extremely good to me, and I was grateful for it. In the months that followed, I went to church quite often, but I must say that I preferred the simpler form of worship in the Presbyterian Church of Scotland and without doubt the 'meat' in the Norfolk sermons was far below that of James Murray's in Tarves.

The village of Weasenham, I suppose, was typical of West Norfolk. My introduction to the Church of England was followed by my introduction to the village pub, of which I approved wholly. The amiability of the pub as against the ferocity of the drinking in many

Scottish bars was pleasing and a symptom, I think, of the more relaxed lifestyle in rural England. The pub was called the Ostrich. It was run by a retired Army Colonel, an old Etonian fallen on evil times. He had got the lease from the proprietor of the Weasenham Estate, one of the Cokes of Norfolk, who I think was a bit short of money himself. Obsessed by his woodlands, he had created a special area in which he had mixed trees with azaleas and rhododendrons which were glorious at their season of the year. But when his son went off to one of the Guards Regiments, the father had the buttons cut off his old uniform in order to reduce the cost of the son's.

In the 1930s you could travel through England and see acres and acres of run-down pasture, tumbledown houses, and an obvious air of neglect. This was taken advantage of by the hardier incomers from Holland, Denmark and Scotland. This is not to say that there were not many able English farmers who survived the slump and kept their farms in good heart, but so bad was it that in West Norfolk, the hedges so beloved by the conservationists were in some cases ten yards wide and spreading. They were certainly wonderful for bird life, but of very little value to the human beings of the area. One of the good English farmers of Lincolnshire, who was also quite a keen hunting man, told me that in the 1930s he had followed a fox for a run of something like five miles below the Lincolnshire Cliff, without seeing any arable land whatsoever.

I suppose the Scots, Danes and Dutch were resented by the local population, but the Weasenham Farming Company was an example of aggressive enterprise, which did a great deal for the countryside in this period between the wars. It was a lesson in reversing decline. The county's farmers had once been in the forefront of the Agrarian Revolution with the four-course Norfolk rotation started by Coke of Norfolk and other pioneers. They had, however, got too comfortable and slack. Such families as the Alstons now got hold of large bits of the county as did the Keiths who had prospered greatly in the eighty years or so they had been in Norfolk.

What turned it back into a decent agricultural country was the introduction of sugar beet. Sugar beet improves the land by throwing down deep roots and, followed by the more traditional crops like barley, gave a degree of prosperity and certainly a lot of work to people in the industry. Brun the Dane also introduced the Weasenham farm company to the growing of grass seed, mainly cocksfoot – another plant throwing a lot of root, which again improved the light soil of the area. At that time it was certainly not monoculture. The rotation of sugar beet, cocksfoot and barley was a very good one.

This was before the days of the combine harvester, but while I did not rate the Norfolk farm workers as comparing with the Aberdeenshire ones, I had to admit that in harvest time they got on with the job. Their regular pay stopped and they were put on a lump sum for the whole harvest. This was essentially piecework. They had a dry climate and I was astonished at the speed with which crops were cleared and again threshed out of the stook and stored or sold straight away. The straw then was not burned but stacked, and I understand that when the War came along, a lot of it went for paper making.

The accountant of the Weasenham Farms Company was a man called Mitchell. He had worked in Aberdeen. For his health's sake he had taken what he thought was this interesting but easier country job in Norfolk. He used to be very amusing about his association with Captain Keith. They were, like any expanding company, always short of money and Mitchell had to adopt a routine to get essential cheques signed. He would start off when Captain Keith (who lived mainly in Northumberland) came down, by getting him to sign three or four cheques. By the time of the fourth cheque a frown was appearing on the face of Captain Keith who had a fairly short fuse, and Mitchell then slipped in a large incoming cheque, followed by one or two more outgoing. By the time they got half way down the pile, Captain Keith would rise to his feet and say, 'Mitchell, I will pay no more to these bloody robbers today.' This primitive method of budgeting certainly worked in their case, as the company expanded and throve.

My motor car, the old Austin 12 Tourer, I disliked more than somewhat, as an impatient young idiot. I prevailed upon my father to lend me £50 for a new car, which I would repay over a year, and I bought a second hand Singer Le Mans two-seater sports car. The price was £45. I probably could have bought it for £40. I was very proud of this nippy little sports car and showed off in it, taking with me Billie Jones who was the daughter of one of the bankers of the company. She had thick black hair and the great thing at that time was to let the windscreen down and the hair stream behind.

I had had the car for about two weeks when I was due to go home for a few days. I then took a bet with Mitchell, the accountant, for the enormous sum of £1 that I would be in Aberdeen inside eight hours, and took off intending to show Lindsay, my future wife, my smart new motor car. I drove far too fast, or as fast as it would go, up to Lanark, just south of Glasgow, where I stopped to look at the signpost. There was a burst of flame from below the bonnet, the whole car was afire in seconds and I had to leap out smartly and pull my case from the boot. I pushed the remains of the car into a field and caught a fish lorry which took me to Aberdeen inside the eight hours. Mitchell wouldn't pay up, and I had to take Lindsay out in an old Ford 10, which was all I could possibly afford to buy. The car was insured Third Party, Fire and Theft, to my great relief.

Although in the end I wanted to go back and farm and live within sight of hills, I enjoyed my time in Norfolk. I was only six months there, however, because on the outbreak of the war on 3 September 1939, I went to Norwich and joined the RAF Volunteer Reserve. The nice recruiting officer at first tried to reject me as I was a farmer, but I knew that he could not, because I was not yet 21. He then tried to persuade me to opt for an Observer's Course, that is Navigator/Bomb Aimer, on the grounds that I would get in earlier for it and I could always change to a Pilot's Course later. I foolishly accepted his advice and as a result delayed my chances of promotion by at least a year and a half.

I finished up with the Weasenham farming company, to the undisguised approval of Brun, the Managing Director, and I departed for Aberdeenshire to await the call to arms. But it appeared that I was not as necessary to the war effort as I thought. The weeks went by with repeated farewell parties. In the interval I went before the Universities Commission Board in Aberdeen. During my interview members of the other services tried to get me to change my mind about the RAF, but I refused. I wanted to fly.

I was recommended for a commission, but it was February 1940 before I was finally called to Cardington. There I was 'fitted' (not quite the right word!) with a uniform, and introduced to the sort of disciplinary NCOs who were plentiful there. I was posted to an Initial Training Wing in Hastings on the south coast. We were put up in one of the empty seaside hotels and started a programme of drill and sport. I went along to the gym where Len Harvey, a former Heavyweight Champion, was the Sergeant Instructor. Seeing I was a large man, he took an interest in me. He showed me how powerful short jabs delivered from six inches away at a rate of about three to the second could be much more effective than my powerful swinging 'hay-makers'.

Soon, the usual RAF disorganisation took over. After only ten days I was posted to another Initial Training Wing in Cambridge. There we were put up in St. John's College. We did a certain amount of armament work, and some training in theoretical navigation, but in the main we drilled and played games. I enjoyed Cambridge greatly and stayed there waiting for posting for flying training until the middle of June 1940.

I did some more boxing under the tuition of an ex-guardsman, Joe Mullins. He was the landlord of a pub called The Volunteer and had been an Army Heavyweight Champion. He said to me one day, 'Mackie, I have someone your size coming down and I want you to do three two-minute rounds with him.' 'Delighted, Joe,' I said, 'I need some competition.' When I arrived at the gym the next day I found a Physical Training Corporal Instructor being rubbed down, and this made me a little suspicious. I became much more suspicious when he put on a head shield, took a couple of smacks at the punch bag, which rocked it considerably, and climbed into the ring.

The bell went for the first round. I was extremely cautious, backing away, and after about a minute of this Joe said, 'Go on. 'it him, Mackie!' I started to mix it and after a few seconds got him a tremendous smack over the heart, which can often be painful. It was a very unfortunate blow because he came after me and knocked me all round the ring. I stayed swapping blows until the bell went. In the second round I was again extremely cautious, and in the third round I was practically running backwards. My neck had been stiffened by a couple of solid punches on the jaw. However, he had not succeeded in knocking me out and by this time his wrath was beginning to cool.

When the bell went, I staggered over to the corner. I said, 'Joe – you bastard, who's that?' He grinned and replied, 'Tom Reddington of Salford. He's fighting Jack London next week!' I may say that Jack London knocked him out in the third round. But after that I realised that even a moderate professional is much better than a good amateur.

The weather in the summer of 1940 was ideal, both for Hitler's invasion of Belgium, Holland and France and for young men living in the beautiful surroundings of the Cambridge Colleges and enjoying the Backs, the river, the pubs and the girls. I met many people from all parts of the British Isles. Nevertheless, it seemed an interminable time as we were all keen to get to flying training. The standard of drill was, I understand, very high, but I cannot say that I particularly enjoyed it. Certainly at no time in my life have I been fitter, as we marched a couple of miles to class and played some form of sport every day. During the Battle of France, we were issued with ancient rifles and sent occasionally on wild goose chases looking for alleged parachutists. I tried to get my transfer to a Pilot's Course, but totally failed and when my posting came through along with others for navigation training on the Scottish west coast at Prestwick in early June, I went off very happily.

I followed the political events with keen interest and, of course, applauded the change of government when Churchill took over. In spite of the enormous success of the Nazi armies, it never entered our heads that we would lose the War. It is now fashionable to decry the rather outdated patriotic stance of the pre-War days, but it stood this country and indeed Europe and the world in good stead. While I myself was an anti-fascist, most of the young men in RAF air crew had a simple patriotic outlook as well as the desire of most young men to go to war and do great deeds.

Later that summer, I was to be found putting down my last two shillings at the dog track in Ayr. I was four miles from home – my digs in Prestwick – but bet it all on a forecast that the first two in the race would be numbers 4 and 3. Sure enough, numbers 4 and 3 won. I thought I might collect enough money to have a pint in the local, The Ayrshire and Galloway. I parked my ticket down at the pay-out window and the man looked at it, but carried on counting out notes. Eventually I said, 'I want paid out.' He looked at me and said, 'You fool. This is for you!' and gave me £28. If you multiply that by only 20, and I think it should be more at today's money, it comes to about £600 and even today £600 is enough to give a young man quite a pleasant time for a while. I was much gratified and I spent most of it taking out a nice blonde girl called Phyllis.

At Prestwick we were billeted out in the town. I had digs with another Aberdonian, Scottie Taylor. We slept in a large double bed and were looked after very well by our landlady. The Navigational School was partly run by a civilian outfit and we had air experience in a Fokker four-engined aircraft. It was the first time most of us had flown, I suppose, but as air experience goes, it was quite useless: no one could possibly be sick in the smooth flight given by the old Fokker. We then went on to have a fairly intensive course of navigation, met. (meteorological) knowledge and a bit more gunnery. We had a number of civilian instructors, many of them ex-Merchant Marine. The Chief Instructor in Navigation was a man called Key who was constantly giving pep talks and encouraging people to study hard in order that they might achieve promotion. But we were there in the summer and it was amiable – lots of girls were on holiday from Glasgow and the pubs were plentiful. We had a really very pleasant time in Prestwick. We certainly did learn a bit, but not under genuine Air Force discipline; we were simply living in digs and on a course of instruction.

Things changed, however, when we were posted to Bombing and Gunnery School at Evanton up in Ross-shire. Evanton was a regular training station. The food was very bad and I don't think, looking back, that it was well run. Our amusements were in Inverness, when we could get there, and in a local pub where we often went to have high tea as against the appalling food in the airmen's mess. We lived in airmen's huts and were subject to discipline by NCOs who disliked aircrew cadets. They knew that we would be promoted to Sergeant or commissioned quite soon, and they rather took it out on us because of this.

We flew in the Fairey Battle and a variety of other aircraft. We did bombing on the ranges and air to air firing. Although it was a fairly easy course, one or two people were taken off at this stage because they were sick doing the air firing manoeuvres. The only indication that I had of my own future was that after creating a tremendous disturbance during a party in Inverness, the Squadron Leader in charge of the Section sent for me and told me that I wouldn't last long as an officer if I continued to behave like that. I was glad to hear I was to be commissioned – and subsequently glad to find that in fact such behaviour occurred quite often in the commissioned ranks.

I went to my father's – and my grandfather's – tailor in Aberdeen, Christie and Gregor, to order my uniform. The proprietor was a Mr Hughes, who was quite a character. Major Keith went in to him one day and said, 'Hughes, I want you to turn this coat.' (The cloth of an overcoat under the lining was obviously in good condition and it was common practice in those days to undo the coat, turn the material to the unused side out and you got what appeared to be a new coat.) Hughes looked at him and said, 'I will not.' 'Why not?' said Keith. Hughes – 'I turned the damned thing seven years ago.'

I had a good leave at home. Then I was finally posted not far away to Lossiemouth where there was an Operational Training Unit (OTU). There, crews were formed of pilots, observers, wireless operators and gunners. At long last I was to be made ready to wage war in the famous Wellington bomber.

CHAPTER 5

War in the Desert

I ENJOYED THE WAR. It sounds callous, but young men do enjoy war and do have a curious attitude to casualties. You have to adopt a cynical approach and an apparent contempt for death. You call it 'the chop' or say, 'The old reaper got him,' and that sort of thing. All quite necessary in a war: the British 'stiff-upper-lip' is quite a good way of people conducting themselves in trying times.

But my first experience of being frightened did teach me a sharp lesson – that when you're in danger, you must do something. That dicey event occurred on 18 January 1941. We had been on a cross-country training flight in a Wellington; came back to Inverness and then flew towards Lossiemouth, about forty miles further, on the east coast of Scotland. We got into a snowstorm at low level and were thrown about in a dangerous manner. I was afraid, and considered prayer. I then suddenly said to myself, 'You have got to do something about it. It is no good just sitting wimping.' I left my navigation table, went up beside the pilot, had one look at him, and saw that this experienced Captain was unsure of what to do and having difficulty in controlling the aircraft.

We had just left clear air and Inverness was still free of snow, so I lifted his helmet flap and shouted in his ear (without using the intercom), 'Turn 180 degrees and fly due west!' He did this on instruments. We came out into clear air just over Inverness and landed at the aerodrome there. We waited a couple of hours until the storm passed and returned to base. One of the other Wellingtons from the unit crashed into the sea in that storm.

I had first arrived at Lossiemouth in December 1940, dressed in Sergeant's uniform. I went to see the Adjutant with a rather vague paper saying I had been commissioned. He looked at it and said, 'You are now an Officer. Put a white band on your arm until your uniform arrives and move into the Officers' Mess.'

For the first time we were now doing some realistic navigation, mainly in Ansons, reliable old twin engined planes. Looking at my Log

Book, I see the records of those three-hour trips: Base/Strathy Point/ Rona/Flannan Isles/Inverness/Base. Sometimes we flew above cloud, and mostly on plots and wind speeds taken by myself.

We then formed into crews by a simple process of self-selection. I met a New Zealand Sergeant called Gilbert Alington and liked him; we crewed up and assembled a Rear Gunner, Bob Turner, from Ayr, a Wireless Operator called Bill Marshall from Glasgow and a Front Gunner, Jim Balfour from Devon. We proceeded to train in Wellingtons, the bombers we would actually be flying on operations. We were put under an experienced Captain who had done one tour and flew with him fairly constantly for navigation, bombing and gunnery.

In general, life at Lossiemouth was extremely agreeable. The Mess was comfortable and well run, and Elgin was a pleasant town. There we did the usual amount of pub crawling. I shared a room with Norman MacIver with whom I had been at both school and university, although he was a year or two ahead of me. I am sorry to say he was later to be killed on his first tour.

We were also given some training, a minute amount, in administrative matters. After one session as Assistant (under training) Orderly Officer, some of us had to take our turn as Orderly Officer of the day, inspecting the kitchens and asking for complaints. I was delighted by the chance to check whether the airmen's messes were run as badly as they were at Evanton. I found that my treatment as a 'sprog' officer by the sergeants in charge of the sections was inclined to be perfunctory. So I made a very thorough inspection of the kitchens and the loos. I found both far from satisfactory and ticked off the NCOs in charge. I put in a very adverse report on two occasions to the Adjutant and I was told that it did have some effect. My experience of bad food in the ranks at Evanton had done me some good.

We were now approaching the end of the course and doing a lot of night flying. On a particularly bad day on 5 February 1941, three crews crashed out of the six. Sergeant Walker's crew crashed in the morning. Four people were killed. The second crew to crash had several injuries. Then Harry Craigmyle crashed at night. Two of the crew were saved from the sea but he and two other crew members were killed.

I had to tell Harry Craigmyle's wife. It was my first experience of casualties. Although Celia Craigmyle was wonderfully brave about the whole business, it did make me realise that wives should not be with their husbands on operational stations. Furthermore, if a captain of an aircraft is living with his wife while on operations and he finds himself at 20,000 feet over the Dutch coast with some small fault showing in an engine, the fact that he has a wife waiting in a warm bed at home is bound to have a negative effect on his decision.

The consensus of opinion amongst the instructors now appeared to be that Course Number 13 was unlucky. We had not quite finished, but it was decided we should be posted to operational squadrons without further flying. I had a good leave first. We all went to a dance in Aberdeen where my wife to be, Lindsay Sharp, partnered Freddie Winsor, while I took the blonde Phyllis – Lindsay had joined the Volunteer Reserves of the Women's Army Auxiliary Force and on the outbreak of war was mobilised and sent to Wick as a telephone operator. There, she was very popular with the young officers of the Fleet Air Arm. But her mother pleaded ill health and got her out of the WAAF. She went to University back in Aberdeen and was doing an MA. We rather drifted apart.

My posting came to 15 Squadron Wyton in Cambridge in 1941. This was a permanent station built not long before the war with a beautiful Mess. I shared a civilian batman with another young officer and never have I been so well looked after. As a very junior Pilot Officer, I greatly enjoyed this treatment: baths were run, buttons were cleaned, tunics were pressed, clothes laid out, drinks were brought – very heaven. (It was to be sadly different three and a half years later when I was to be back there on my third tour sharing a Nissen hut in which I had the NCO's room. We were looked after by a WAAF batwoman who was too busy handing out her favours to the junior officers to waste any time on an elderly Squadron Leader of 24.)

We were allocated an aircraft and had some more fairly intensive training. Flight Lieutenant Curry was, of course, an experienced pilot, but I had to make absolutely certain that my navigation was as up to date as possible. This was done by night flying cross-country over England. We also dropped practice bombs using the same bombsight on which I had been trained at Lossiemouth. There were differences in the equipment on operational aeroplanes on which we had to gen up. By the time we set off on our very first operation, I regarded myself as a fully trained Navigator/Bomb Aimer, although events were to prove me not quite correct.

A large number of barges had been assembled in various ports for the German invasion of the British Isles. Although the danger had receded since the Battle of Britain, they were still considered an important target. On 26 February, we went to bomb barges in Boulogne. This was a regulation first trip for new crews and should have taken a maximum of three hours.

However, when we got there, full of excitement and anxious to destroy large numbers of barges, we saw the cone of searchlights going up into the sky and made our way up to the target. The nasty cunning Germans put the searchlights out, thereby totally confusing eagle-eye Mackie. I could not see the outline we had studied so hard before take-off. So we went round again and each time I think the Germans played with us, although at one point a searchlight did flash over us.

We did five runs. On the sixth attempt, I suddenly saw the harbour very clearly, and the barges strung out across it – a perfect target. We did a classic run in and I released the bombs and saw them straddle the barges. We then went home to find Wing Commander and Station Commander about to go back to the Mess thinking another raw crew had bitten the dust.

However, they listened with great care to our exposition of precision bombing and we went off out of the Ops Room very pleased with ourselves. As we left we passed a large scale map of the French coast on the wall and there I saw my target clearly outlined – the exact shape I had bombed. But it was not Boulogne, it was Le Touquet. I am ashamed to say that I did not speak a word about it.

We were now considered ready for operations proper. Our first target was Cologne, where we went on the night of 3 March. This was a good deal more exciting. There was lots of flak, we were caught in searchlights and there was very much an operational air about it. Again we saw the outline quite clearly, and on the first run I was able to bomb the target point. But we saw two of our aircraft burning on the ground on the way out, thanks to German night fighters.

The appearance of more and more of these night fighters, plus an incredible concentration of anti-aircraft guns, searchlights, scare flares, diversion targets laid out in open country, and the best radar the Germans could bring to bear – these were all sure indications that the enemy was diverting any amount of material and men in defence of their Homeland.

We next had an abortive operation to Kiel; we abandoned it after 35 minutes because of possible engine trouble. Our next one went to Hamburg. There we were badly caught in the searchlights, and I had my first experience of being rocked by anti-aircraft fire. But we got through it and again we bombed the aiming point. When we got home, we found that we had about eighteen shrapnel holes in our aircraft.

In March we went to Lorient, in South Brittany, where there was a submarine base. We were laying mines against submarines. We landed back at St Eval in Cornwall because of fog at base, and had to wait until afternoon before our base was clear. At lunch time I had a couple of pints of cider, thinking this was an innocuous drink. It was the first time I had tasted the real stuff and when I got up to go to the loo, although my head appeared perfectly clear, my legs buckled under me. However, by the time we took off, I was able to do some navigation.

We went on leave then and when we came back we found that Flight Lieutenant Curry had been posted to another station as a Squadron Leader and Sergeant Alington became skipper of the aircraft. We did another trip for new crews to Calais. It only took the three hours, as by this time we knew the form and bombed the barges successfully in the right port.

There followed an epic journey to Malta, the Mediterranean island then under continuous aerial attack from the Nazis. We had been put down to take aircraft out to the Middle East to reinforce the bomber group there. Extra tanks were fitted in the ten Wellingtons for the long flights and we were issued with tropical kit and sent down to Hampshire for take-off. It was an interesting experience preparing: the planes were so burdened with additional petrol, we were severely limited as to the weight of travel baggage we could carry.

The route was over France to Marseilles and thence over the Mediterranean to Tunis and the Gulf of Hammamet and then straight to Malta, 200 miles further on. We had been training very hard for this and my rear gunner had been very useful, taking drifts over the sea. We threw out a flame float behind us: the rear gunner then sighted his bank of four guns on it. He read off its calibrated bearing. The difference between that and the supposed direction of our course showed how much the wind was pushing us out of line. This gave the navigator the drift, which allowed me to make that amount of correction to the course.

Bob Turner had been very good at taking drifts over land and water. Then he had gone to the Gunnery Leader and asked for reassuring instructions on the process for our long flight to Malta. The idiot Gunnery Leader told him to take a sight on the flame float and then follow it for a minute and gave the navigator the difference between the readings. This was rubbish.

We hit the French coast with a clear pinpoint and set course for Marseilles. I was getting drifts from Bob, all reading nil or one degree, with the result that I thought we were dead on track. About the time we were due to hit Marseilles, I went up front and was standing looking out with the pilot when he said, 'There are funny clouds ahead.' I looked at them for a minute. 'They aren't clouds, them's Alps! Steer due west!' So we turned away from the Alps, steered due west and within ten minutes came out over Marseilles, which was all lit up, and, with a sigh of relief, set course for Tunis.

We set out two flame floats and each time mistakenly thought we were dead on track, when far ahead of time we hit a coast running north and south, and turned towards it. I had a good look and saw an aerodrome below and a fighter take-off and I suddenly realised that this was Sardinia. Again, we set a fresh course. By this time we were very late and it was broad daylight. We hit the Tunis coast, flew across Tunis and set course for Malta. We then received a wireless message broadcast to all aircraft coming in, that the enemy were approaching Malta from the north. The Germans at this time were raiding Malta constantly from Sicily, which was only half an hour's flying away.

We had already been in the air for about nine hours. Bob Turner, when he heard that this message, had come over, panicked a little and said over the intercom, 'For fucksake, Mac, send for a fighter escort.' All the fighters in Malta I think had been shot down at this time and this was gloriously irrelevant. I sternly told him to be quiet and keep a sharp look out, and returned to my navigation. This obviously had to be spot on to hit Malta in the middle of the Mediterranean. We were extremely short of fuel. We broke wireless silence and asked for directions to steer from the Malta base. There was now nothing much that I could do, so I went back to the astrodrome to keep an additional look out for fighters. We were flying low over the sea.

Suddenly out of a cloud came a Messerschmitt 110 which proceeded to put in a rear attack. He came at us to about 300 yards, opened fire, and we saw the tracer coming across. Bob, by this time absolutely cool, held his fire until the Messerschmitt was at 200 yards and starting to break away, and poured several hundred rounds into his belly. He disappeared into cloud and happily we did not see him again. We were told by radar in Malta that he had disappeared from the plot and obviously been shot down into the water, but Bob never got the credit he deserved from this victory.

Shortly afterwards we saw Malta, with the sharp outlines of small fields, and we were certainly delighted. We landed and taxied to a dispersal point. When we got there one of the engines conked out, short of fuel. Although there was no damage to the tanks or to any vital communications, we had two or three holes in the aircraft from the fighter. The geodetic construction of the Wellington, being interlaced aluminium spars, made it very resistant to damage – many Wellingtons took a terrific amount of hammering and made it back to base.

One of the pilots stationed in Malta during this period was a flying officer called Topham. He had done a tour in the UK during which, while bringing in a damaged aircraft after a raid, he had written off the Chance light (a big light used to illuminate the runway to assist pilots landing at night). The next thing that happened to him involved a cheery girl in the town, known as Toppy. He was in bed with her one afternoon; during an air raid, a bomb hit the block and removed one wall of the building. Topham and Toppy were left safe in bed, but the chair with Topham's uniform had disappeared. He borrowed a skirt of Toppy's and ran to Admiralty House in the centre of town, into the magnificent ante-room which housed the officers' mess and, dressed as he was, had several large whiskies.

He was considerably shaken and subsequently in Egypt went rather to pieces. I was Orderly Officer there one day when the CO, Turkey Rainsford, came to me and told me to place Topham under close arrest in his room. I went into the bar to find him slouched in a corner chair muttering, 'Get some ops in!' and other totally undeserved remarks to the Group Captain and the Wing Commander who were having a very forced conversation with each other. The only thing I could do was pick him up in my arms and carry him out. As we passed the senior officers (studiously talking shop), Topham threw his arms round my neck and in a loud voice shouted, 'Mac, you'll help me against these bad bastards.'

He was court martialled in Cairo. Plug Lodge, an officer in 70 Squadron who was a lawyer in civil life, defended him, and Turkey and I had to attend as witnesses. We gave our evidence and then listened from the next room to Plug Lodge defending. He pled unsympathetic treatment of a brave but shaken officer. His peroration ran like this: 'This officer has carried out many operations – he brought 13 tons of blazing metal in to land in Britain and in Malta he was the sole survivor of a bombed house.' One of the members of the court had been shaken in a raid recently and Topham got off with a light reprimand. He was taken off operations and posted to ferry aircraft from Takoradi on the west coast of Africa to Cairo. The Takoradi run was a sought after posting. Pilots could buy a python skin for £5 in Kano or Ma Dugri and sell it in Cairo for £50. So virtue was rewarded.

From Malta we took off that night in the middle of another air raid and flew across Libya to the Nile delta which we had to cross in daylight. For young airmen who had never been out of the country before, this was a fascinating sight. The sudden transition from flying over the Western Desert to this fertile delta, fertilised and watered by the Nile, was doubly appealing to me, both as a farmer and as a rather tired airman. The sharp green of the irrigated fields was easy on the eye after the brown desolation of the desert.

But by this time, we were weary and snappy with each other. We landed at Abu Seweir after four hours flying and slept for ten hours. Abu Seweir was a permanent station. We stayed there in some comfort for a couple of days and investigated the very pleasant little town of Ismailia, on Lake Timsah at the top end of the Great Bitter Lake.

The Heavy Bomber Group in the Middle East – our destination – operated from advanced bases in the Western Desert. We were posted to a tented transit camp near Geneifa. This was extremely uncomfortable and, although it was only just May, very hot. Happily, we were only there for a few days before being posted to 148 Squadron, flying Wellingtons from Kabrit at the south end of the Great Bitter Lake and right on the Canal. 148 Squadron was part of 205 Group, which consisted of four squadrons stationed on the Canal – two squadrons, 70 and 148, at Kabrit and two squadrons stationed at Geneifa.

The Wing Commander of the squadron was 'Sparrow' Lewis and the Flight Commander of A Flight, Squadron Leader Wells, was known as 'Kong' Wells because of his hefty appearance. He was moved shortly after to command another squadron. The new Flight Commander was a South African called Bush Abbot.

We lived in some comfort. Apart from the heat, we had pleasant rooms and an Egyptian bearer to look after each officer. It was here I first made my acquaintance with the chatty. This was a rather porous earthenware vessel which held our drinking water. It was suspended outside and the evaporation seeping through the earthenware made the water surprisingly cool. Kabrit was a very pleasant permanent station and well-equipped.

But in May 1941 the situation in the Mediterranean was deteriorating. Wavell had routed the Italians, taking enormous numbers of prisoners, and advanced beyond Benghazi, thereby securing the whole eastern seaboard of the Southern Mediterranean. When the Germans invaded Greece, it was considered a point of honour, although militarily incorrect, to reinforce the Greek army which had also done extremely well against the Italians. This resulted in greatly weakening the situation in the Western desert, where German troops had also arrived. An advance was taking place which would retake the whole of Libya to beyond Tobruk. The Germans were successful in conquering Greece and later in conquering Crete. This ebb and flow in the Western Desert finally resolved in 1942 after the Battle of Alamein. Montgomery received enormous logistic support and this, combined with the British/American invasion of North Africa, gave him advantages that other more brilliant commanders had done without.

On 20 May we did our first operation, the first of many to Benghazi. The procedure was fairly complex. We were briefed initially at Kabrit, then took off with a full petrol load for an advanced landing ground, in this case LG109, which was just beside the town of Fuka. There the planes were bombed up and topped up with fuel. We took off at 2300 hours and flew straight across the desert to Benghazi, bombed and flew back. Benghazi was a main supply port for the Axis troops, and we visited it constantly and, I think, quite successfully.

We used to attack from six or seven thousand feet and occasionally made a sweep at a lower altitude. Although flak was fairly intense over the target and there were some fighters, the operations were more comfortable than over Germany. The main trip was more boring than anything else. One of my navigator's logs was subsequently pinned up in a navigation officer's office as an example of what not to do. The log was supposed to be a complete record of the flight, changes of course, height, pinpoints and landfalls, so that at any time mistakes could be found and corrected. On it I had put, 'Took off LG60, 2300 hours, bombed Benghazi 0300 hours, landed LG60 0600 hours.'

My logs were not always quite as bad as that one. But navigation was easy, in that I had by this time properly instructed our rear gunner in taking drifts. We would throw out a small incendiary bomb over the desert, take a sighting, and normally hit Benghazi on the nose after a three-hour flight. It was also easy to tell when we arrived, because there were always a few clouds on the coast and in the clear Mediterranean air one could identify the target very easily. As we had not any real aids, it did depend very much on map reading. If things went wrong, then one could always use the sextant to take a shot on the stars, which were very much clearer on the Mediterranean.

I settled down to a routine of flying up to the Western Desert to one of the advanced dromes and flew mainly to Benghazi or to Greece or Crete. The most interesting of the landing grounds was at LG60, which was in fact a salt pan or dried up lake, about 60 miles south of Fuka Satellite. The surface was absolutely perfect and much smoother than any runway. We were once delayed there for three days waiting for a spare part and had a most enjoyable time exploring the desert, chasing a gazelle in a jeep, and finding all sorts of interesting ruins, including a Roman well 100 feet deep. This gave me a taste for the desert and I even considered, after I had finished this tour, applying for a posting to the Long Range Desert Group. Operating deep behind enemy lines, it appeared to me to be an exciting prospect.

When the Germans invaded Crete our bomber group – four squadrons of Wellingtons – was on constant stand-by to bomb the German forces landing there by glider and by parachute. But the intelligence was extremely bad and we never seemed to take off at the right time. We could have put over forty aircraft in the air, and if we had had the correct intelligence as to whose hands the aerodromes were in, it could have made a tremendous difference to the campaign.

As it was, our squadron did one or two good raids – we did one on Heraklion and blew up an ammo dump – but most of the time we were held back. Sometimes we took off and then the operation was cancelled. Sometimes we got up to the desert and waited a day before we did anything. All, I suppose, part of the fog of war. But it was very upsetting for the crews, who knew they could do much damage if they knew where the enemy were. The Germans took Crete eventually and, apart from some supply dropping to the brave men in the hills who were holding out and waging a guerilla war against the Germans, that was the end of that.

We did, however, go up the Aegean to Greece quite a lot. Our aircraft was part of an excellent operation to block the Corinth canal. It meant going in at low level and dropping 1000 lb bombs into the opposite side of the steep walls of the canal. We were successful and the canal was blocked for a long time, thereby hindering the German communications greatly. Other members of the group went in at nought feet to the harbour and dropped mines which put the harbour out of action.

With my CO, Turkey Rainsford, I did a marking operation, a path finding operation to the oil tanks at Piraeus. This was really most successful: we dropped our incendiaries right over the tank farm, thereby lighting the whole thing up for the rest of the group going in after us. We did a bit of damage.

Coming back from that particular operation, Turkey left the pilot seat and handed over to Dagwood Watson, flying as second pilot. He went back to the astro hatch to look around. He had no sooner plugged in than he let out a shout, 'Tracer over the starboard wing,' and shot past me up into the cockpit, where Dagwood Watson had already started to take evasive action. A few seconds later a calm voice from the rear said, 'Rear Gunner here, Sir. That starboard engine has been giving off sparks for some time.'

Flying over the Aegean and Crete at night was a glorious experience. We normally flew in full moon, as fighters were not particularly competent or plentiful in that area, and the islands, Crete itself and Melos and Leros, in Mediterranean moonlight gave an absolutely wonderful impression. I always swore that I would go back after war finished and take a boat round the islands for a year – though I never did.

Social life was limited to mess life really, but we did get quite a lot of leave. In Cairo, we did the usual things that young officers on leave do: drank too much, drove around in a gharry shouting our heads off, had dinner and then went to the Casino Badia where we drooled over the luscious creatures abounding there. On our first leave in Cairo, we put up in a decent hotel, the Carlton. I was accompanied by a friend, Dickie Millburn, and two New Zealanders, Phil Fougere and Neil Blundell. We were delighted with the food and Neil Blundell went off to the New Zealand Club. We joined him there later and found his eyes sparkling because he had found imported New Zealand Waitemata beer.

The next day we started in Shephard's Hotel and then went to see the Pyramids and prepared for the journey by camel ride by soaking up many drinks in the Mena House Hotel. We then rode by camel to the great Pyramid and, as you were allowed to do at that time, climbed to the top and took photographs.

Alexandria, too, we found fascinating. We once took off from there by compass during a sand storm when we had to be back at base for operations that night. Fortunately for us, the compass was correct and when we got airborne in a very few feet, we were up above the blinding sand and into clear air. This sort of thing would never be allowed today.

I went to Tel Aviv with Dickie Millburn – a haven of civilisation, with good cafés and hotels along the waterfront, all rather German, but extremely enjoyable.

But I think the most fun we had was in Ismailia. There was a very pleasant United Services Club and we could sail on the Great Bitter Lake and enjoy the French and Greek Clubs as well. I once met an old friend who was a sergeant, and for some reason we couldn't take the United Service Club boats out, so after a drinking session in the Greek Club, we hired a boat at the public pier. I set off, with Brydon Webster and Neil Blundell extremely drunk in the bottom of the boat and myself at the tiller. We got out into the lake, sailing before the wind at a good pace, when the other two decided to swim to sober up. A good idea, I thought, and they dived over the side.

I was spanking on, enjoying the breeze, when I looked round and all I saw were two dots in the far distance. I had then to beat back to collect them and wasn't making much of it when I spotted a very smart dinghy, sailed by a chap I vaguely knew, an Army Major, and shouted to him to pick up my two friends. But they refused to be picked up, and he pushed off, with me shouting abuse at him. When I finally got them into my boat, every time I went about and swung the boom over, one of them was knocked into the water again. Eventually I placed them firmly in the bottom and we somehow got back to the pier. There was a crowd of excited Egyptians waiting there. We got out and no fewer than two extra people demanded payment for the boat which we had already paid for. They didn't succeed.

Although flying these operations in the Middle East was easier than over Germany, we lost a lot of people – very good ones. The weather was responsible for quite a few because we were operating a fair way from home, in old-fashioned aircraft. Severe icing did occur over the hills in certain conditions. Bush Abbott, a very popular flight commander, was lost I think because he pushed on through ice and then was shot down by ack ack over Greece. Bob Gordon, a really first class operation pilot, was lost over Derna when the Fleet Air Arm dropped a flare at too great a height. It made him a perfect target for the ack ack, and he was shot down with his whole crew, including a very nice young fellow called Bitmead, a farmer's son from the West of England. I well remember Bitmead listening with tears in his eyes to one of my old friend Freddie Winsor's gramophone records, 'I Found My Thrill on Blueberry Hill', for there had been a Blueberry Hill quite close to his home.

Freddie Winsor himself was the epitome of a joyful, carefree, but competent chap. To bring that gramophone and his collection of about 500 records, he had ignored the instructions on our heavily-burdened flight out to keep our luggage down to a minimum. All his gramophone records were a great joy to us when we eventually got to Kabrit. Anyhow, Freddie Winsor bought it too. Freddie was shot up, and he crashed trying to make his way back. All the crew were killed.

We received the first 4000 lb bomb in Egypt. Turkey Rainsford decided that he would drop it. He took me with him as he thought I was a good bomb aimer. It was an interesting experience. We loaded up the bomb at Kabrit, but as we took off an Egyptian truck drove across the runway. Turkey swerved and hit the sand, slowing us down. But he pushed on at full throttle. I was in the astro hatch for take off, which I suppose I shouldn't have been – I well remember fear making sweat spring out on the palms of my hands.

We laboured off, just making it over the Bitter Lake. Having started to climb over the Delta, however, one of the oil gauges fell rapidly to zero. Turkey had to make a decision then as to whether it was simply the gauge or something severely wrong, and he decided he couldn't risk proceeding. We had to turn back to base at Kabrit watching the gauge and watching the engine. We also had to dump some fuel before we landed and, although it wasn't an operation, I must say that I landed full of relief that it was over, as did Turkey. It was a curious thing – as soon as you happily touched down, you forgot all about it. We did drop the 4000 lb bomb on our next operation on Benghazi and thought we hit the target, which was shipping in the harbour.

At Kabrit we shared the aerodrome with a Special Service Group who did parachute training and a detachment of the Royal Navy. The Navy were extremely friendly and often in our Mess, because we had a supply of pre-war Plymouth gin. When the gin ran out, they did not appear quite so often. The parachute training went on fairly constantly in the area and Dickie Millburn and I asked if we could do a drop. We arranged to go down, operations permitting, and jump with some other trainees. However, the day before, they had a very nasty accident. A row of parachutists were jumping out on a static line. One man jumped and the static line failed to open his parachute. The second man hesitated and the instructor barked again, 'Jump!' Such was the training that he jumped and he too was killed. This episode obviously shook us a little and Dickie and I were very glad that the next day operations were on after all, and we couldn't jump.

The station was commanded by Group Captain Joe Fall who had been a Fighter Ace in the Royal Naval Air Services in the First War and had no fewer than three DSCs. He was Canadian, and a considerable character. We had a visit on the station from the famous Alice Delysia, the First War music hall star. She sang her famous song, 'J'attendrai' and, although to us she was an old woman, she came over as well as ever and we all loved it. She came to the Mess afterwards and Joe Falls was drooling around her. We could not understand why this old man (circa 47) could be behaving in this way.

Although the War was going badly, with the fall of Greece and Crete and the advance of Rommel in the desert, morale was extraordinarily high. I do not recall any defeatism and certainly none of the attitude portrayed in *Catch 22* and other books of that sort. We were all there to do our duty and most people were content with that. Many of us enjoyed the excitement and comradeship, and we were looking for the bubble reputation in the cannon's mouth.

Nevertheless, although operations were much less wearing than those over Germany, there was a certain amount of strain, even amongst those who were excited by action. It showed itself in a variety of ways, mainly by small mannerisms such as constantly stroking one's moustache. There was a vogue for big moustaches in Egypt and it was, of course, excellent moustache country in that they seemed to grow well in the heat. I met one fighter boy in a nightclub in Cairo whose moustache you could see on both sides from behind. I grew quite a bushy moustache, but when I got back to Britain, it had to be trimmed. I found that at the sort of altitudes we were flying in, it froze on my oxygen mask.

We had one rather unpleasant episode at Kabrit, concerning rifle drill for the aircrew. Although irrelevant, drill was not a bad thing if kept within bounds. Aircrew had a great deal of time on their hands when they were not flying. But when Turkey Rainsford was away in Cairo one hot afternoon, the Adjutant foolishly ordered rifle drill. Thereupon a sergeant, from Australia needless to say, marched up and said, 'I am putting myself under arrest.' Most of the sergeants did the same and we had what could have been called a mutiny. Turkey came back from Cairo and the thing was sorted out without ridiculous measures being taken. But Turkey believes it told against him for future promotion.

I got on well with the Australians on the station and we played a good deal of poker. We used to play in the empty morgue. It had emergency lighting, so that we were not irritated by the lights being turned off because of air raids, which were fairly frequent at that time. One one occasion, two Australians were betting against each other – a young chap called Carrol and an older man called Duigan. Carrol eventually threw in his hand and said, 'I will show you what I am throwing in.' He had four Kings. Duigan looked at him and said, 'That is good poker.' He turned over his hand which was four Aces. Carrol had that extra sixth sense which I believe that all poker players need, as well as the ability to calculate the chances. I myself proceeded fairly nicely until a Canadian called Alexander cleaned me out of £20 one evening, whereupon I decided that as this was in fact about a month's pay, I had better take it easy.

My own crew came off operations after carrying out more than the requisite number. I wanted to continue, however, because I enjoyed Egypt and wanted to go on flying. First of all I flew with a Sergeant Pilot called Richmond, who wasn't considered to be quite up to it, to make a report on him. I did a couple of operations with him. While he was willing and not at all lacking in desire to operate or to attack the enemy, I also found him altogether too careless. His crew had no real admiration for him, although they liked him, and he just wasn't sufficiently good to be a captain of aircraft. I was quite willing to take him on if they made me Captain, but there was no precedent for an Observer being Captain in that area of the war.

I did a few more ops with Flight Lieutenant Tommy Piggot, who came from South Africa. He was very experienced, quite senior, and very competent. Then there was a move to collect American aircraft called Liberators and Turkey Rainsford, my CO, thought perhaps I had done enough. He put me on the draft to go home for this purpose.

After a riotous farewell in the Mess, we assembled in a truck and drove to Suez. There we piled on a crowded train for Cairo. I was the senior officer in charge at the elevated rank of Flying Officer. A number of us had to stand in the corridor and we passed the time by taking pot-shots at objects in the desert with our revolvers. Inside the carriage there were a couple of nurses and a young ground staff Pilot Officer just off the boat. The nurses did not like the noise of firing. The young Pilot Officer, rising to the occasion, went to put a stop to it. According to Harry Burr, one of our chaps who had got a seat inside with them, he met me with a smoking Smith and Wesson in my hand, opened his mouth, thought better of it, and dived back into the carriage. He was ashen faced, and said not another word.

We got to Cairo, put up near the aerodrome, and had the usual two or three days trying to get some sense out of Middle East Head-quarters. Eventually we boarded a Dakota to be flown to Lagos. We were delighted that it was a Pan American plane because we knew they had great experience. Walking out to the plane with the pilots, however, we thought they looked remarkably young and not very competent. They told us, 'Oh no, we are not Pan American pilots. We're Air Force pilots, but we were not good enough for combat, so they put us on flying Dakotas.' This hardly raised our confidence.

We stayed the night in what had been a College, on the banks of the Nile just north of Khartoum. We came straight down from 10,000 feet to land. When we got out, it was like stepping into an oven, and each of us had to stop for a bit of acclimatisation before going down the steps. But the evening on the banks of the Nile, after really rather a good meal, was magical. There was a full moon and all the noises of the tropical night. Sadly, there were no beautiful women about – or indeed any women at all.

We flew on next day over the waste of Central Africa to Kano in North Nigeria with two stops to refuel – one at Elfashir where they had a tame lion pup, who later took a distinguished visitor's ear off, then over to Maiduguri. We spent the night in Kano and visited the bazaar. I bought some ebony heads to take home. We then flew to Lagos where we were put up in the Grand Hotel. The hotel did not live up to its name, but there we saw a traditional west-coaster, who had taken to drink. He staggered down in the morning and ordered two large gins. He then shakily put a napkin round the back of his neck, and with one hand holding the napkin, he took hold of the glass with the other hand. He exerted a pull to bring the glass up to his lips and thus steadied the shaking hand. After two gins he was able to convey the rest of his breakfast to his mouth. Although this kind of thing was one of the legends of life as it was on the west coast of Africa, I would not have believed it if I had not seen it.

We spent a fortnight before getting a boat. Although the hotel was bad, we had a pleasant time. The service club had a swimming pool. But we were well warned to keep away from the native girls. (In the tropical night you used to hear them below the trees, 'You come with me, white boy.')

Eventually we embarked on the SS *Batory*, a Polish liner fast enough to proceed unescorted. Happily Montgomery's edict banning drink had not yet gone out and the voyage was enjoyable. As far as one was able to judge, we went practically to Brazil before heading north almost to Iceland and turning down into Glasgow – a route designed to keep us clear of U-Boats. In fact one of the pocket battleships was in the Atlantic at the time and we had a number of scare stories about its whereabouts. We had to take a turn on guard on the anti-aircraft guns but, apart from that small duty, we had nothing to do except exercise, play cards and drink. I shared a cabin with a fighter boy who had been wounded in Malta. We were both sound asleep after a congenial dram when the alarm went off. We grabbed our lifebelts, and found we could not get through the door. It was the wardrobe door we were trying to get through.

The warm nights in the tropics were very beautiful and I suppose we would have paid a great deal of money for that sort of cruise in peacetime. But when we got back to Glasgow there was no going home. We had to report to Air Ministry. We were looking forward to a spot of leave, then training on the Liberators, before flying them back out East. I had greatly enjoyed my time out there. However, when we got to the Air Ministry in London we were informed that we were 'operationally tired' and must therefore become Instructors at an OTU.

Our protests were unavailing, and we retired to a resort much favoured in London by airmen on leave, the Regent Palace. There we proceeded to drown our sorrows. A friend of mine, Dudley Farmer, was a regular officer whose family lived in Kensington, and he had been in the Middle East for four years. In the cocktail bar he met a most attractive girl and spent the next three days with her, alleging that as his family had not seen him for four years, they could do without him for a while longer.

I was eventually, after a round of the usual RAF incompetence, sent to the Cotswolds. There I became an Instructor, a position for which I was totally and completely unsuited.

My grandfather John Yull with his favourite mare Rattlin' Jean and a foal.

My mother, aged 14, proud on her new pony.

My father and mother at their wedding in 1907.

Willie Cumming, my father's manager, who progressed from being a farm servant to becoming laird of a fine 400 acre farm

An early picture of the young Mackie at home in Aberdeenshire.

The house at North Ythsie.

The redoubtable Miss Chalmers and her class in 1927 – Mackie third from right, back row.

George and Lindsay, aged 19.

Our wedding at King's College Chapel, Aberdeen in May 1944.

Farm men at North Ythsie in 1924 – five horsemen with the grieve, Sandy Milne, nursemaid, and sister Catherine.

Officers of 148 Squadron, Kabrit; Mackie third from right, back row.

*My first crew – Gilbert Alington, J. Herridge, Mackie, Bill Marshall,
Jim Balfour and Bob Turner.*

61

My last crew – Steve Atkin, Mather, Mackie, Dewar, Giles, Joe Rafferty and Len Meyden.

Investiture at Witchford in 1944 – medals gained in the Squadron over twenty months.

CHAPTER 6

Stirlings and Boscombe Down

IN THE COTSWOLDS we had a number of rowdy parties at the Edgehill training unit, as well as working fairly hard at instructing crews who were due to go to the Middle East. We were now into the summer of 1942 and the countryside was glorious. We used to go to Shipton-on-Stour where, as usual, we found an admirable pub. Called the Bell, and run by Dickie, Esme and Freda, it was a home from home for us. My friend Maurice Hartford had also been posted to Edgehill: he was in charge of messing and found country house gardens still being run, producing wonderful vegetables and fruit for the neighbouring big houses. I would imagine that we ate more healthy food at that time than in any other RAF mess. I remember Murray Hobbs, Taffy Evans, Donald Dunn, Alistair Lang, Methvyn Leyshon and Peter Way, who was the Squadron Leader in charge. He was a competent Commanding Officer. However, he was also an amusing character whose favourite saying on the morning after the night before was, 'Life is no longer a bowl of cherries, nor yet is love a dancing thing.'

After a particularly rowdy party in which I played a leading part, I was sent for by the chief instructor, Wing Commander Lane. He told me that I was no use to him. He wanted Instructors who did not wish to go back to operations, but he said, 'I am not sending you back.' I thought he said, 'I am sending you back,' and broke into profuse thanks, whereupon he interrupted me and said that if I did a Bombing Leader's Course and came out with good marks, he would post me to any Squadron I wished. I happily accepted this offer and went on such a course at Manby.

We were at the start of the Harris era, which was I believe a major factor in the eventual defeat of Germany. Faced with Nazi control of the whole of Europe, Churchill found that Bomber Command was the only way of striking back at the triumphant Third Reich. Night bombing was still technically uncertain because of the problem of navigation in bad weather but radar and other devices were rapidly overcoming this difficulty. When Air Marshal Harris took over as

Commander in Chief of Bomber Command in 1942 he initiated a system of area bombing. The aiming point was the industrial area of a city, although inevitably the bombs spread very widely. There were large numbers of civilian casualties which we most deeply regretted, but they were only a fraction of the savage slaughter of the innocents by the Nazi regime.

During my time instructing, I had already gone on three operations with the Thousand Bomber Raids which Harris initiated – the first one to Cologne on 30 May 1942, the next one to Essen and the last one to Bremen. Drawing on training aircraft like ours as well as squadron aircraft, these 1,000-bomber raids did such damage that priority was now being given to the production of more such bombers and the training of more bomber crews.

Formally, Bomber Command was responsible to the Chief of the Air Staff and the Directorate of Bomber Ops in King Charles Street, London. However, it must be said that under Harris, Bomber Command had a large degree of influence in political circles, and not only through the Air Ministry.

Under Bomber Command at High Wycombe itself there were various groups. Each of those groups was under the command of an Air Officer and there was a certain amount of competition between them. Two Group, which was a light bomber group, later split off to become Second Tactical Air Force. Three Group started with Wellingtons, went on to Stirlings and eventually, thank goodness, to Lancasters. Four Group was in Yorkshire; Five Group in Lincolnshire; Six Group, who were Canadians, mostly in the Yorkshire area; then, later in the War, the Pathfinder Group, Eight Group, was formed. There was also an immensely complicated system of radar, Observer Corps and other parties. Each individual Bomber Command Station was commanded by a Group Captain. Under him he had a Squadron Leader for Administration and a Station Adjutant. They were responsible for cooking, cleaning, electricity, sewers, medical care – everything.

In terms of flying, there were one or two Squadrons, each under the command of a Wing Commander. The relationship between the Group Captain, as Station Commander, and the Wing Commanders was one of direct command, but of course, with a great deal of individual control by the squadron commanders on whom the morale of the squadron depended.

Each squadron had two or three Flights under the command of

Squadron Leaders. In each Flight, you had 12-15 aircrews and aircraft. The ground crews were under the charge of a Flight Sergeant, normally one trained at the RAF Engineering School Halton – all men of high calibre who had provided most of the Engineer Officers on squadrons and stations. In the Squadron structure also you had Navigation Officer, Gunnery Leader, Wireless Operators, and under the Station Commander you had Flying Control, which had evolved from one Sergeant Pilot giving the OK for take-off or landing to a complex organisation under specialist officers.

The Officers' Mess had its President of the Mess Committee and Bar Officer. The Sergeants' Mess had a similar organisation. The corporals had a room to themselves in the NAAFI and the airmen had the NAAFI and the YMCA and the local pubs.

I quite enjoyed my Bombing Leader's course and came back from Manby ready to begin my promised operational posting. Wing Commander Lane was as good as his word and posted me to Lakenheath in Suffolk, part of Three Group. My Commanding Officer at Lakenheath was Wing Commander Michael Wasse, a good operational type, if tense.

Unfortunately, the aircraft were Stirlings. They had not fulfilled their initial promise. It was very difficult to get them above 12,000 feet, a lethally low height with the strong state of German defences at that time. For enormous efforts were being made by the Germans to counter Bomber Command's attack on their heartland; German bomber production was reduced to produce more fighters and, in an immense drain on both industrial resources and manpower, anti-aircraft weapons were being concentrated all over Germany. The losses of aircrew incurred by Bomber Command alone were to be over 55,000 and comparable numbers were to be lost by the American 8th Air Force. Survivors still reckon that the losses were not in vain but these were the heaviest casualties of any operational force.

I found to my pleasure my friend Maurice Hartford already in the same squadron at Lakenheath. He was going great guns, well into his second tour and commanding B Flight. I did a few operations with Maurice, including one to bomb the city of Hamburg. On an operation with him to Lorient we returned on three engines. As it was the starboard outer engine which had cut dead, that meant a tremendous strain on the pilot. We had to tie a rope to the rudder bar and pull to assist him to keep the plane on the straight and level. We also had a great deal of icing and electrical storms. It was altogether a most unpleasant trip.

Because of my experience, I was to be Captain of Aircraft and got a crew therefore from OTU, captained at the time by a New Zealander, Pilot Officer Ellis, a very good young man. He reluctantly accepted that an experienced observer would be Captain. By that time it had been decided to restrict the use of Stirlings to short range targets and to use them mainly for mining. Mining in fact was a fairly hazardous job, but a very useful one in containing the U-Boats and helping in the Battle of the Atlantic. I did a couple of successful such operations as Captain with Ellis as pilot. Then Ellis went to the Commanding Officer and said that he really would now like to be Captain. I hasten to add that he thought I was a very good captain, but quite rightly he wanted to captain his own aircraft. After doing very well, Ellis was later shot down and he was killed.

On our Squadron we had Flight Sergeant Middleton, an Australian who had been at one time a buckaroo, riding the perimeters of their immense cattle stations. He got a Victoria Cross posthumously for extraordinary endurance, bravery and leadership in bringing a Stirling back from a raid to Milan, although badly wounded. He nursed the aircraft to the south coast of England. It was so badly damaged that he could not have controlled it for a crash landing and he baled the crew out of the aircraft. I am not decrying the rest of the crew, but Middleton deserved his VC if only for the way that although severely injured, he dominated the situation. The crew baled out as commanded, including two officers. The little front gunner, a scruffy Glaswegian called Mackie, stayed with Middleton to help and went into the sea with him.

From the sublime to the ridiculous: we were in a pub in Cambridge where the Assistant Provost Marshal – a form of policeman – was an MP called Gifford-Fox. He was constantly berating aircrews for their behaviour in Cambridge, from the safety of his office. In the pub this night he attacked the Russians, saying that as far as he was concerned, Germans and Russians killing each other was OK by him. Maurice Hartford and a New Zealander called Doug Newall resented this, and waited until he went outside. They pulled him round into a back street and removed his trousers. They then took the trousers back to Lakenheath where they were met by Michael Wasse; he said that he had had a furious telephone call describing them, and told them to go to bed. We heard no more of the incident. I wrote a piece of doggerel which ended:

Beware, MPs of traitorous views
Lest you too, should lose your trews.

The new AOC of Three Group, Ralph Cochrane, now arrived from Training Command, determined to make his name and to do new things with his group. He therefore planned a raid with fresh tactics. It was an extraordinary plan for an operation. Three Group and their Stirlings were to take off on raids to pin-point factories isolated in forests, and were to surprise them by crossing the Dutch coast very low at below 1,000 feet, flying over enemy territory at that height, find the factories, destroy them and return home – hopefully. Maurice Hartford disliked the operation. He said so to Michael Wasse, but, as Flight Commander, put himself down to fly that night, in spite of his misgivings. Or rather, he did so precisely because of his misgivings.

It was three hours later that Flying Control were notified that Hartford's aircraft was already back over the English coast and was coming in to land early.

He told me the story afterwards. As instructed, they went in to the Dutch coast at under 1,000 feet. They were coned and caught in searchlights. He turned back out to sea where he started to climb to cross the coast at their usual height. As he climbed he started to consider the whole operation and got angrier and angrier with this new AOC who was playing with people's lives and disregarding experienced advice. Maurice then decided that, as Captain, he considered the operation ill-advised and unprofitable to continue, whereupon he jettisoned his bombs in the sea and returned to base.

Maurice Hartford at this time was an experienced operational pilot on his second tour, with the DFC and an excellent record. He reported what he had done to Wing Commander Wasse, who agreed with him in principle, but not in practice. Wasse said to him, 'I am certain Cochrane will raise hell and try to have you court martialled. For God's sake, Maurice, let us say you had an electrical fault or engine failure and returned because of that.'

Maurice refused and stuck to his guns. Wasse had no other option but to report it to Group Headquarters, whereupon he was told to place Hartford under arrest until action could be taken in the morning. However, long before morning, it transpired that Three Group's losses on this occasion were some 30 aircraft out of 90, one of the highest percentages ever recorded in a bomber operation. No more word was heard of the court martial.

Afterwards, Maurice and I discussed his rejection of the AOC's orders more than once. There was one argument against his conduct – if a man like Hartford does this it may well save a number of lives and improve the practice of command, but it then encourages lesser men to make the same sort of judgment and the rot can spread very quickly in an area of high casualties. He eventually said that perhaps he ought to have gone on with the operation and, after coming back, put in an extremely adverse report. But I always maintained that his action was correct. My reason was as follows: the action in a man of proven courage and experience had the dramatic effect intended, and I had no doubt that it took a great deal of moral courage.

But it troubled him for a long time. He always maintained that, had I been Captain, I would have gone on with the operation. I think that this was possible. However, when one does an operation like that and returns safely, the relief at getting back is such that one's moral indignation evaporates; and so it might well have done in the case of Maurice Hartford. The other, and greater, likelihood was that the protest would have been lost because he would never have come back at all.

Cochrane survived his criminal mistake and went on to receive great praise as a senior commander, but Hartford was posted as a Test Pilot to Boscombe Down, the main experimental aerodrome for the RAF on Salisbury Plain in Wiltshire. Although he greatly enjoyed it, this was unjust. He should have been allowed to finish his tour (God willing), when undoubtedly he would have received a DSO. By this time, as I was a close friend of Hartford's, I think I was bracketed as a trouble-maker. I suppose I was, in that I was at the stage of over-confidence in my experience, to the extent that I doubted the judgment of my commanding officers. I was also offered a posting at Boscombe Down as Experimental Bomb Aimer, and accepted it.

While we were together at Boscombe Down, Maurice proposed that we go to Ireland on leave and look up the remains of his family home which had been burned at the time of the Troubles. He was flush with money, having just inherited two thousand pounds from an aunt, and agreed to lend me the necessary cash as I was already on overdraft. In the summer of 1943 we motored up to Holyhead and took the boat to

Dublin. When we got to immigration, Maurice produced his relations and was let through. Immigration asked me if I had any relations in Ireland. 'No,' I said, 'I'm Scots, pure and simple.' He looked at me and said, 'Why are you going to Ireland? You can't go unless you have your nearest relation there.' Whereupon I replied, 'I hear Dublin is a wonderful place to go on leave.' He looked at me, grinned and said, 'You're dead right, boy. On you go.'

We did indeed have a wonderful time. The Shelbourne Hotel, where we stayed, was admirable. Breakfast normally consisted of kidneys and a pint of Guinness, and then we got round Dublin. We found the racing restaurant, the Dolphin, where they had wonderful steaks set out for you to pick yourself. To meat-hungry carnivores, this was a glorious opportunity. Along with the steak we found that they had a Chambertin 1928, which was absolutely delicious. We never had fewer than two steaks a day and with each, of course, a bottle of the admirable Chambertin. The people of Dublin were really all extraordinarily friendly. We were instantly recognisable as young Brits on leave, and people would actually approach us and ask us out for drinks, and indeed to dinner.

One extraordinary incident took place after about a week when Maurice said we must now see if anything was left of his family house, Rose Court. We hired a taxi and drove to Port Arlington, about forty miles from Dublin, stopping at the occasional pub on the way. We went to the Garda (police) station. They were extremely helpful, and told Maurice that Rose Court was indeed no longer habitable. They did, however, say that at a rather nice Georgian house in the middle of the street a man was living whose mother was a Hartford. Maurice went up to the door, and said, 'Good afternoon. My name is Hartford.' The woman looked at him and said, 'I can see that. Come in.' Maurice was taken upstairs to where her husband was ill in bed, while the taxi driver and I went to the pub. After a while Maurice reappeared, as the taxi driver and I were on our third pint of Guinness, and told us the story.

The couple were living in obvious straitened circumstances, but the husband had insisted on giving Maurice the actual uniform and the shako that Maurice's great grandfather had worn at Waterloo. He had also given him two pictures. Maurice protested, but he replied, 'No, no. I am not a Hartford. You are the last of the Hartfords. You must have them.' The pictures revealed why the lady instantly recognised her caller. One was of a woman whose hair, forehead, eyes, nose, and big, dark eyebrows, were exactly a replica of Maurice's. When Maurice got back to the UK, he had the pictures valued and at that time they were worth about £700, which would have been an absolute fortune to the couple. There's great style about the Irish which is very endearing.

After he finished giving us this account in the pub, Maurice went over to an old chap in the corner and said to him, 'Did you know the Hartfords?' But the chap looked at him and said, 'The black Hartfords!' Then he spat. So we reckoned it was time we went back to Dublin. We stopped once more at a pub en route. The taxi driver and I had ordered more Guinness when the door burst open. In came Maurice dressed in his great grandfather's coat and shako, saying, 'If I can't wear RAF uniform in Ireland, I will wear the uniform of Waterloo.' In about five minutes, the pub was full of curious people and an enormous party ensued.

We got back to Boscombe Down exhilarated, if not much rested. While Farnborough did the more original sort of research and experiment, Boscombe was the practical station for testing RAF aircraft. The heavy bomber test flight was B Flight and the armament testing was C Flight. Maurice Hartford was posted to B Flight, where he immediately made his mark as an exceptional pilot. He undertook the first Empire Test Pilot's course, coming out with high marks, as he had an admirable mathematical brain.

I went to the armament flight which was concerned with the testing of new bombs and bombsights. The bombs varied from the 12,000 lb blockbusters to the roly-poly bombs used in the Dam Raid, and incendiaries. I arrived in late January and immediately started work on incendiary bombs. After the German success in setting fire to East London, they became more and more important in Bomber Command.

I greatly enjoyed the summer of 1943 there. I see from my log book I flew in Hampdens, Bostons, Mitchells (an American plane), Halifaxes, Wellingtons, Lysanders, Lancasters, Vigilants, Mosquitos and Ansons. I stayed until early September. We had an interesting selection of people at Boscombe Down. We had the scientists and the mathematicians, whom we lumped together as boffins, and a variety of aircrew, mostly pilots who came from Operational Commands and Training Command, but who were all specialists in their line. In my particular section, we had a flight lieutenant, at least he was dressed as a flight lieutenant, called Carrier, a good chap and I understand an extremely able mathematician. He really was a prototype boffin; such was his interest in any of the aeronautical subjects requiring his attention that he would require a pilot to do the most dangerous things, while he, as a passenger in the aircraft, was totally absorbed in his subject. Happily, the experienced pilots were able to redirect his more curious experiments and thus preserve both him and themselves.

He lived in a remote cottage with his wife. She was pregnant, and one morning he came into work and said, 'My wife had a baby and I think I did everything right according to the book, but perhaps I should have the doctor to see her.' His astonished friends agreed with him. When the doctor got there, he said that all had been well done, and happily there had been no complications.

I became quite expert at hitting low level targets with skip bombs and incendiaries. With an experienced pilot flying at the same speed and with a mark on the perspex, flying over familiar ground, one got to know exactly when to press the button. 'Professor' Carrier, as we called him, designed a low level bombsight and was rather hurt when I told him that I spat on the perspex to give me an aiming mark. We dropped these bombs at various locations, including Porton, where large concrete aprons and walls were erected for this type of work.

I was very successful with low level bombing, but much less so with high level. The Minister of Home Security had a large square of concrete on pylons erected at Ashley Walk and various bombing aimers before me had tried to hit it, in order that the effect of armour piercing bombs on many feet of concrete could be gauged. None of them succeeded, and no more did I. We were supposed to hit it from 20,000 feet and at this time we had not got the new RAF bomb (SABS) sight which was as good as the American Norden. The authorities sent a lead crew in the US 8th Air Force, who had just finished a tour, to try, captained by an admirable pilot, Russ Schleeh. They dropped two or three sticks of practice bombs and then with the real bombs hit the target smack in the middle, much to my delight mixed with a good deal of chagrin.

Maurice Hartford and I became very friendly with Russ Schleeh and we took him round the local pubs in the valleys running through Salisbury Plain. There we discussed weighty matters of aeronautical warfare, inter-planetary travel and the sort of things that slightly pretentious young men do. On the third night we were in the back garden of a pub near Boscombe Down, and having a fascinating discussion over our third pint when Russ Schleeh suddenly looked at us and said, 'Say, don't you guys ever think about women?' Whereupon we apologised profusely and took him into the Cathedral pub in Salisbury where women abounded.

Russ Schleeh went back to the States and became a test pilot at Wright Field where Maurice Hartford met him again. He was a wholly admirable American who had been through the roughest period of the development of the 8th Air Force. They lost a great many people in developing daylight raids over Germany, and indeed to start with they had many losses when they were raiding the French ports and other targets. When ready, they proceeded to fly deep into Germany, but could only do so when they had long range fighters capable of escorting them. Even with this, the losses were very heavy. They were much more dependent on people like Russ who were the lead crews, and very often when the lead aircraft was shot down the bombing degenerated from high level accuracy to wild releases of bombs over the wrong targets. The losses of the 8th Air Force were enormous, as in Bomber Command.

During the winter, I played rugby for the station team and I remember an epic battle with a Welsh battalion stationed on Salisbury Plain. It was one of the toughest games I ever played, but when we finished it became amiable. That summer, what I really enjoyed was being a member of the station cricket team, playing village teams in the valleys, always beside a pub, and on occasions some kindly man would bring you a pint as you stood on the outfield. I was a rotten cricketer and I had never really enjoyed the game before, but the way it was played that summer appealed to me greatly.

In the autumn I heard my old friend and Commanding Officer, Turkey Rainsford, had got a Squadron of Lancaster IIs. The Lancaster II had the air cooled Hercules engine. Compared to the way we laboured off the deck in the under-powered bombers to which we had been accustomed, these immense engines were to make take-off a joy. I rang Turkey up and asked if he would give me a crew and perhaps a flight. He replied, 'Yes. Come along.' I was to find myself bombing Berlin.

CHAPTER 7

Lancasters

I T STILL FILLS ME with a sort of fearful nostalgia to recall that extra-ordinary first sight I had of Lancasters going into action. Having arrived in Norfolk at Little Snoring, I booked into the Mess, walked over to see Turkey Rainsford and had a long chat. By that time it was fairly late in the evening and he said, 'I am just going down for take-off. The boys are operating tonight.' The mission was one of the few at that time being done in moonlit conditions. We drove down to the runway. It was just at the exact moment of moonrise that the flight of Hercules-engined bombers took off. I watched while each big Lancaster flew one by one in silhouette across the full moon's rising face. It was an amazing sight.

My own first operation in Lancasters a few weeks later was not, however, to prove to be a long story. As Captain Bomb Aimer, I was standing beside the pilot when we took off into the Norfolk darkness in Lancaster F for Freddie. It was 2000 hours on 7 November 1943. We had 12,000 lbs of mines loaded on board and we were proceeding to the mouth of the Loire to lay them in front of the Lorient submarine pens. But we were just off the ground when one of our four engines – the starboard outer – cut dead.

We did a vicious swing, just clearing a cottage and some trees, hauled back the throttles and bounced back across the aerodrome. We retracted the wheels after the first bump to bring her down on her belly and she came to rest with the engines on the starboard wing burning, in the middle of one of the Dispersal Points where aircraft were parked out of the enemy's way. I opened the top hatch and exited in a hurry. Then I remembered I was supposed to be Captain of this aircraft and had better see the crew out. I went along the fuselage via the top hatch and the pilot, Steve Atkin, went along the inside. We helped the crew out of the centre top escape hatch. I realised that I had left a new peaked officer's cap on the Navigator's Table. It had cost me £3.17s.6d, and I went back for it. But in my hurry I fatheadedly left a camera on the table which as loot would have fetched £100.

The aircraft by this time was burning quite nicely. The foam buggy with the fire crew arrived and almost succeeded in extinguishing it. But then the foam ran out and the flames proceeded to spread. By this time Wing Commander Rainsford had arrived. He judged the situation to be getting dangerous and sent everyone off. But he and I stood watching for a little while, hoping the fire engine would be back in time to put it out. When the fuselage itself caught ablaze I said to Turkey, 'Don't you think we've been British for long enough?' He agreed and we departed quite hurriedly in his Hillman staff car. We raised our speed considerably when, as we were still only about 200 yards away, the entire plane blew up.

The explosion did a great deal of damage to several Lancasters parked round the Dispersal Point although otherwise the blast behaved in the usual curious manner, doing little harm on the aerodrome but breaking windows three miles away in Fakenham. The only casualty among us at the time was Sergeant Joe Rafferty who had scratched his face on a gorse bush. Otherwise I was unhurt and so were the crew. They were to fly with me on all my subsequent Lancaster operations.

I had got this crew on my arrival at 115 Squadron ten weeks earlier. They had just been posted to the squadron. Flight Sergeant Steve Atkin, the pilot, was a very brave man. He had been injured in a crash while training and had come back to get on to operational flying. He readily agreed to fly with me as captain and the rest of the crew appeared to be very happy with the situation. The navigator was Sergeant Mather, a nice West Country boy, the wireless operator/air gunner was another West Country boy called Giles, the mid and upper gunner was the Irishman Joe Rafferty and the rear gunner an Australian, Len Meyden, who had been a musician – both classical and dance – in Sydney. The front gunner's name was Balfour. He was English, and our flight engineer was Dewar, also English.

We did the required training together at the Conversion Flight, some miles away from Little Snoring. It was manned entirely by ex 115 Squadron people and some of them were extremely good. The main Flying Instructor for Steve Atkin was a New Zealander, Bob Rogers. Pilot Officer Rogers was extraordinary. He looked like a gorilla, with enormous hands, but he had the most delicate touch of any of the pilots there. Exploiting the great powerful Hercules engines in the Lancaster II, when on air test with minimum petrol and no bombs, he could feather three props and even so, climb a little on one engine.

(Feathering means turning the angle of the propeller blades absolutely parallel to the main fuselage and cutting out the engine.) He was also a very good Instructor and gave Steve Atkin a lot of confidence in the Lanc II. On our first solo a prop ran off and had to be feathered. Steve did everything correctly and landed on three engines, which was an excellent omen for the future.

The crew welded together quite nicely and I had been looking forward to our first operation. We joined the Squadron in late October and did one or two country flights for familiarisation. But then followed our disastrous abortive mission to the mouth of the Loire on 7 November which ended with F for Freddie exploding on the airfield.

After such a crash on take-off, it was obvious that the quicker we completed our first operation, the better. We were briefed for Berlin. We took off successfully this time, Steve Atkin remarkably steady in spite of his previous experiences, and set course over the North Sea. But then things went wrong again. The navigator got into a complete muddle and took us a long way off course. He did not appear to me to be able to take us on to the target on time, so I decided that, in view of the general upset to the crew, it would be right to abandon the operation. We jettisoned our bombs and came back to land.

I explained my reasons to Group Captain Sim and he agreed that after the experiences of the crew, it would probably have been wrong to go on. But he finished with a steely look and said, 'See that it doesn't happen again.' The expression at Bomber Command at that time was 'the chop', and after our crash on take-off and our first abortive operation, the crew were becoming known as a 'Chop Crew'. In the circumstances of a Bomber Command Squadron bearing heavy losses, this sort of thing was understandable and very difficult to combat.

A couple of nights later, we were briefed again for Berlin. It was always a time of tension before an operation started, but it helped that we were kept busy with preparation and seeing all was right with the plane. We went out to our aircraft and awaited the order to start up and taxi to the runway. Take-off was at intervals of under one minute and, as our heavily laden bomber gathered speed, tension was inevitably fairly high. And concentration on getting off and into the climb was not confined to the pilot. By 1943 the Germans were sending 'intruder' fighters to attack bombers over their own aerodromes, both on take-off and landing back, and a sharp lookout had to be maintained. I watched several bombers shot down on approach to their home base after a successful raid, and it seemed doubly sad.

This time I saw that everyone in the crew was right on top line, and keen to eliminate the feeling of fear induced by the series of incidents leading up to this operation. All went well and we secured a photograph of the aiming point. It made a terrific difference to the morale of the crew. We went on to do another eight or nine Berlin trips in a row, all of them successful. Our reputation then changed from being a 'Chop Crew' to being one possessed of immortality.

Len Meyden was a very bright Australian and a good and cool rear gunner. We got on extremely well and I was delighted when he and Steve Atkin were commissioned towards the end of my tour. Steve was an above average pilot and we too worked extremely well together. We developed excellent co-operation in the air. We consulted about tactics; the ultimate decision was mine as Captain, but as pilot he had to act quickly and independently in situations of crisis such as a fighter attack or being caught in a searchlight cone. We never had a disagreement in the time we flew together.

On one trip, for example, on the way to Berlin we got into trouble with icing. We couldn't get above cloud hampered by the ice, so I decided we could drop off some of our incendiaries to enable us to climb. I went down to the bomb bay, set the distributor which selected the bombs, opened the bomb door and let them go. There was a sudden lurch and we shot up through the cloud layer. I realised that our big 8000 lb blockbuster had gone. I closed the bomb door and went up beside Steve, pondering my boob and whether we should go all the way to Berlin with two canisters of incendiaries. I realised that I had to go back to base and face the music. 'Okay, Steve, turn round – we're going back,' I said. All this time, Steve hadn't said a word, but then he said, 'I thought you'd never make up your mind.' (When we got back, I found that a new procedure for release had been instituted and while all other bomb aimers had been instructed, Mackie had not. It was put down to mechanical failure, but the laughter on the station had to be borne.)

We were coming out of Berlin one night in January 1944, when two Lancs collided in front of us. It was at the turning point, where the stream of bombers was altering course to the west. One exploded immediately, and went down in a ball of flame. Steve Atkin shouted to the gunners to look away in order to preserve their night vision. The other plane in the collision did two upward rolls ahead of us with all four engines burning, and blew up at the top of the second roll. After we landed back in England the mid upper gunner, Joe Rafferty, asked what the big glow had been. When told, his knees buckled and he almost hit the deck.

Coming out of the target at the turning point was always a time of danger. When actually over the target too, there was great danger of collision. The Squadron consisted of three Flights of 12 or more Lancs, often putting over 36 bombers on operations, and in order to reduce the effectiveness of anti-aircraft fire and searchlights, the attack on targets was concentrated within a very short time.

I dare say that, on the whole, this concentration of planes on the route and over the target was justified, particularly from a point of view of marking by the Pathfinders and massing bombs on the ground. But by this time, the German fighter tactics were also well worked out, and in spite of various anti-radar devices, they normally got into the stream of bombers. It certainly gave the fighters a tremendous chance, particularly as they knew that the underbelly of both Lancasters and Halifaxes was undefended, and many German fighter pilots evolved deadly techniques, scoring up to five victories in a night. It was extremely expensive for us in aircraft and crews.

Nevertheless, looking at my log book, I find that we did a total of 11 operations to Berlin. This was a period when Bomber Command had nearly perfected the Pathfinder technique, and really did an immense amount of damage in the German capital.

The sight of great cities burning, the ack ack, tracer, flares and searchlights, with bombs bursting on the target, is one which I will never forget. It signalled a successful operation and another strike at the heart of the evil Nazi empire. We knew that our bombing was causing tremendous civilian casualties among the German population, but we also knew that there was no other way at the time. Looking back, I find it astonishing in my career as a Bomber Captain, as an Experimental Bomber Aimer and as a Staff Officer, that the techniques of waging war took over my preoccupations so much. One found it fascinating to discuss the methods of fire raising so as to engineer great blazes between the sites of the different explosions, and the moral considerations did not enter one's head.

Thinking of this nature must, of course, have taken over the minds of many people who were in the sort of desperate situation we found ourselves in from 1940 onwards. The much-maligned Air Marshal Harris summed it up brutally, but correctly, when he said, 'I do not believe a German city is worth the life of one British Grenadier about to cross the Rhine.'

It is difficult to convey to people living sixty years later what a very close run thing was the Second World War. Hitler bestrode the whole continent of Europe and had willing assistance from many of the satellite and conquered countries. The scale and intensity of the German defence of their homeland against the bomber crews was enough to assure us that the bomber policy was effective and worth the losses to ourselves. It is fashionable today to decry what Bomber Command did, but there is little doubt that the enormous diversion of effort to defend the German homeland was a major factor in enabling the Russians to hold out, and eventually to counter attack – and was in fact an effective 'Second Front'. German production of bombers slowed to a trickle and their efforts concentrated on fighters and on 88 dual purpose cannon which mainly went to an anti-aircraft role. Albert Speer, who was in charge of reconstruction, had no doubt whatsoever that the efforts of RAF Bomber Command and the 8th Air Force of the United States of America were the major factor in the defeat of the Third Reich.

But we aircrew were indeed suffering heavy losses. During this period, the likelihood of a crew finishing their first tour of 25 operations was small. While I was on the Squadron, from October 1943 until May 1944, only 7 crews out of 30 did so. We were losing about a crew a week. As a result, the keeping up of morale was all-important and in the circumstances, it was extraordinary how high it remained.

It depended very much on the Flight Commanders and second tour 'veterans'. The only way was to have a certain form of black humour about 'the chop'. We moved to Witchford, near Ely, where a third C Flight was formed and I was put in command of that, with the rank of Acting Squadron Leader. One night, as CO of the Flight, I came in to sign the Authorisation Book. I found – placed there, of course, by my 'friend' and second in command, Flight Lieutenant Halley, a Newfoundland Irishman – a large axe lying on the book with its blade underlining my name.

One had to swagger a bit. I did not like Berlin as a target any more than anyone else, but when on Berlin, I always made a show of coming back from the first briefing whistling, with a pleased look on my face, which at least amused the crews, who knew that that meant we were going to 'the big city'.

It was true too that drink played a large part in keeping the tension down. It was quite noticeable that on operations, nights off relaxing over many pints of beer did a great deal for the nerves. I only knew one teetotaller who seemed to remain calm throughout a tour. Of course, how much he really was calm and relaxed, no one knew.

I deliberately fostered an impression of uncaring indifference, but like everyone else, particularly when we had to rest before a late take-off, I found it difficult to sleep and many times wondered why the hell I was doing this, when I had already flown a good number of operations and could well have remained on non-operational duty. However, once one actually took off, then everything had to be concentrated on the job in hand. And of course, the subsequent happiness of returning home was complete.

I once saw a badly damaged American Forces bomber land at an emergency runway on the Norfolk coast – the crew got out and kissed the runway. We were amused but we knew how they felt. I think one of the most trying times for a bomber crew was if a tank had been hit and fuel was short. A similar situation arose if the aircraft had been shot up and damaged, possibly with some of the crew wounded; the alternation of hope of getting back and fear that you wouldn't made the toughest veterans tense and fearful. The pleasure on touching down was unlimited.

I remember sitting in the darkened control tower one night trying to keep order. I was there because someone with flying experience always had to be on such duty. A young WAAF who was sobbing was instructed abruptly to keep quiet. The Commanding Officer of B Flight, a youthful New Zealander called Baigent, was late back from a raid on Berlin and we had no message. Then faintly over the radio came a voice which said this was B for Baigent. 'May I come straight in?'

'Of course,' I said, and he landed to the cheers of the people in the control room, which I was quite unable to prevent. The plane was badly damaged but skilfully handled. One crew member was wounded, and another was to claim a wound stripe because a bit of shrapnel broke the skin on his bum. Baigent turned off in front of the control tower and said, 'May I stop here? I am a little shot up.' I immediately said, 'Yes.' He put on his brakes, and came to a halt. Part of his wing immediately fell off.

This episode was regarded by all the aircrew as a proper example of nonchalance and understatement. Baigent received a Bar to his DFC, and we had many such examples which were of immense value in keeping up the morale of the ordinary crew.

During the period of the intensive bombing of Berlin I had one trip in the spring of 1944 in which the Pathfinder techniques went badly wrong. The outward route was over Denmark and into Berlin from the north; the route home was supposed to be safely north of the Ruhr to the Dutch coast. By this time, I had had a good deal of experience, and as I had little to do with flying or navigating the aircraft, being Bomb Aimer Captain, I got to know the ground over Europe fairly well. I was lying in the bomb bay, looking for pinpoints, and I realised as we got to the Danish coast that we were off course.

We worked out a fresh course from the pinpoint I gave the navigator, calculating that the wind differed from that originally broadcast to us. We came in from the north over the coast on the correct turning point and went into Berlin along with the Pathfinders. We bombed the aiming point and got a photograph, turned round for a look and then came out on the given route. From over 20,000 feet one could see the distinctive shapes of the searchlight groups round the German towns. In particular, Hanover was egg-shaped and very noticeable. I was able to give the navigator approximate positions and we came out on track, north of the Ruhr.

But we could see the main stream, off course, flying right through the Ruhr, getting shot at with everything they had. When we got back to base, the Navigation Officer back-tracked our log and found that we had been smack on the recommended course the whole time, and reported this to Group and Command. I complained about the inaccurate winds we had been given. The reply came back that Mackie should have flown through the Ruhr with the rest of the stream. I could see the curious logic of this, but in actual fact was very glad that we were on our own as otherwise we too should have had the attentions of the German fighters and the heaviest ack ack in Europe being directed against us.

There was always a tendency of Group Commanders to be extremely jealous of the Pathfinder forces. I do not think the previous episode had much to do with it, but at this time 3 Group decided that they would pick some crews of their own to act as Master Bombers. I was selected, and we did training at low level around Britain. Then we set out to attack a V2 missile site in northern France. This appeared to work, and I found that as Observer Captain, I was able to direct operations probably rather better than a pilot could have thanks to the tremendous co-operation Steve Atkin and I had developed.

We did a further attack on the marshalling yards at Villeneuve St Georges. This was highly successful too as only one stick of bombs fell outside the target area. We did another one on Frederickshaven on the Swiss Border, after the United States 8th had missed the target. That also appeared to be successful. I was feeling very pleased with myself, and looking forward to developing this technique for the rest of my tour.

Every squadron in Bomber Command had its favourite pub. In our case, it was the Cutter Inn in Ely down by the riverside. Mrs Wenn was all that a landlady should be – plump and cheerful and extremely nice to 115 Squadron. When the pub shut, we would stay as long as we wanted – she used to produce fresh bread and cheese and pickled onions, most of which came from a sister who had a farm in the Fens. It was at the Cutter that I had a celebration party with my crew when my DSO was awarded for an accumulation of operations in Europe, Egypt, Greece, and culminating in the several successful Berlin raids. It is true to say that medals play an important part in the motivation of young officers in wartime – I was pleased with the fact that I was awarded the DSO as a Flight Lieutenant, still a Junior Officer – and it helped morale in my Flight and on the Squadron. (A DFC came later, on completion of my last tour, after some successful master bomber operations.) Mrs Wenn gave us beautiful vegetable soup, followed by a delicious roast goose, followed by a trifle, followed by cheese and we had a very cheerful, happy evening. The next day I went down to settle up my bill. She looked at me and said, 'Do you think that half a crown each would be too much?' She was really a great joy and delight, and had a great deal to do with keeping up the morale of the Squadron.

The announcement of my DSO appeared in the Scottish papers and Lindsay wrote to congratulate me. We had been going our own ways for four years, and I seized the chance to arrange to meet her. The old attraction fired up again, and we soon decided to marry. When we got engaged, Lindsay often came down from London and stayed at the Cutter. On one occasion she was met at the station by some of my friends, who said nothing about me, took her to the Cutter where she had some supper, then stayed there drinking and having a party, still without a word about me. Lindsay kept quiet, never once asked, 'Where's George?' and at 12 o'clock they raised their hats and said, 'Lindsay, George is over Berlin!'

I went back to the Cutter some years after the war. Unfortunately, Mrs Wenn had died, but Mr Wenn and the son were running the pub which had been refurbished by the brewers in the worst possible taste, with a lot of the beautiful mahogany covered up by coloured Formica.

It was very nerve racking to live a reasonably normal life in modest comfort and then proceed from that two or three times a week into mortal danger. But I have always been proud of the way morale in Bomber Command kept up in the face of the heaviest losses of any service. The number of cases of breakdown appeared to me to be quite small.

Aircrew who refused to fly were sent for classification, and if categorised as lacking in moral fibre (LMF) were stripped of their rank and put to ground duties. I do not think that this system worked well. Very often the clever dodger of his duty was able to give the answers which the examining 'trick cyclist' wanted, though I knew of cases where I had given sympathetic reports, indicating that the airman concerned had tried, but simply could not make it, whereas people whom I knew to be scoundrels bluffed their way through interrogation. There were, however, very few.

Great figures like Guy Gibson and Leonard Cheshire were immensely important, as they set standards which could be aspired to, if not equalled. But everything ultimately depended on the tenacity and devotion to duty of the captain who, although he was part of a large number of bombers, proceeding under orders to a target, still had the authority to abandon the attack or press on in face of difficulty. There was a great responsibility on the senior members of the Squadron – few, if any, of whom exceeded the age of 30.

Funnily enough, some of the best discipline in the air came from Australian captains who were extremely disrespectful of authority while on the ground. One British crew who came to my flight, as soon as they were allocated an aircraft, took the ground crew out on a pub crawl and got drunk with them on that very day. It was difficult to impress upon young skippers that ground crew and aircrew had to earn each other's respect and reward and that bribery was not the way to do it. Obviously you could not run aircrew like recruits to a Guards regiment, but a certain insistence on sensible discipline and dress helped the Captain to keep on top of his crew when in the air.

I had been expecting to get command of A Flight when 'Stopper' Grant, a Canadian, was posted in to take it. He had been on Blenheims, a light bomber which suffered savage casualties during the Battle of France and whilst attacking Dutch coastal shipping. He had survived one tour and after a spell in Training Command was coming back for a second tour on heavy bombers. We got on extremely well and became very friendly, although he alleged that, such was my thirst for promotion, he saw a gleam in my eye when he was down to operate! He was married to a charming girl whom everyone called Sweetie. I knew that he really did not have a great desire to operate, but he felt it, of course, to be his duty to do a second tour.

In a drunken moment, our Irish doctor told me that my own attitude had a bad effect on 'Stopper' for he envied what appeared to be my lack of worry and my confidence that I would survive. Bobby Annan, an old friend from my days in Egypt then commanding the Squadron, asked my advice on taking Stopper off operations and posting him back to training, as he was obviously a bit jittery. I was shocked beyond measure, and said to Bobby, 'You can't do that to him. He would never forgive you.'

I was, of course, a bloody fool. Stopper would have gone to a non-operational job without any disgrace and with a good deal of relief, but such was my attitude at the time that I really thought it would be quite wrong for his sake. He was to be my best man if he could get leave. But a week before I was due to be married he was shot down and killed on a trip to Aachen. This distressed me greatly, not only because of the simple loss of a friend, but because of what I had done.

It was in March of 1944, when I had got engaged to Lindsay and was looking forward to finishing my crew after 25 'Ops', that I myself was sent for by the AOC Base. I was told that, as I was on my third tour, I was myself to finish after a total of only 20 Ops. I protested strongly – indeed rudely – whereupon the AOC, who was a kindly and clever man, said, 'Calm down, Mackie. The thing is that we have got to watch morale and if a chap with your seniority gets shot down, it hits morale very badly. On the other hand, if you finish your third tour, particularly with your number on Berlin, it does morale a great deal of good.'

Secretly, I suppose I was rather relieved. I had flown in total more than 75 operations. I hoped that my pilot Steve Atkin would have reasonably easy trips for his own last five due operations. But then, with only three more operations to go, he and the crew went down too, over France, and all were killed. We suspected it was due to our own bombs falling on them from above.

Joe Rafferty, the mid upper gunner, was the one who had buckled at the knees some weeks earlier when realising that the glow in the sky over Berlin had come from two of our fellow Lancs colliding. He was older than the rest of the crew and he had always been a good Irish Catholic. Joe was going off to Mass one day and I jokingly said, 'Joe, you can pray for us.' I thought I had been rather insensitive when he replied earnestly, 'I do, I do, I always do.'

Joe also had more conventional RAF superstitions. When they were 'missing believed killed', I got a sad letter from his girlfriend, in which she wrote that Joe always said, 'I'll be all right as long as I'm with Mackie. No Hun will ever get him.' I have those devastating letters from mothers, wives and sweethearts to this day, and it has been appalling to think that whilst I continue still hale and hearty, my Lancaster crew have all been dead for over half a century.

CHAPTER 8

In the Air Ministry

IN MAY 1944 I left the Squadron and my career in Lancasters. I was flown up to the nearest aerodrome to my home by a Lancaster crew doing an exercise. Lindsay was in Aberdeen making all the preparations for our wedding but I arrived back at North Ythsie and promptly went to bed with high fever. They thought it might be a recurrence of sandfly fever, exacerbated by stress. However, fortified by a couple of large whiskies, I did stagger up to the altar in King's College Chapel, in Aberdeen. Lindsay said that when I turned to greet her, she was nearly knocked over by the odour of drink.

The wedding service went on quite happily and, and we had a teetotal reception in the Northern Hotel. It was alleviated by the fact that there was a bar next door. Lindsay's mother, Mrs Sharp, was President of the British Women's Temperance Association. (I may say that in her later years she became very fond of a glass of sherry, with, when she had a cold, even an occasional spot of whisky.) We went off by train for our honeymoon in Killin in the heart of the Perthshire Highlands. Killin was beautiful, though I suppose it would not have mattered if we had gone for our honeymoon to Wigan.

I was then posted to the Air Ministry, to Bomber Operations, the department which controlled Bomber Command. As we had access to the War Room – underground in the basement of King Charles Street, and connected by passages to Downing Street – every day we could follow progress of the armies in Europe. There was a long slog to break out of the Caen Falaise situation and then the exciting sweep up through France, the capture of Paris and the much harder battles before the Rhine. The 51st Highland Division was in action from the start and as I had many friends in the 52nd Lowland Division who had been trained for mountain warfare in the Highlands of Scotland for three years, I waited to see when they would appear on the map. Their first action was in fact below sea level in Holland.

I was in Bomb Provisioning. This entailed co-operation with the other departments. It also meant a certain amount of co-operation with the War Office and the Admiralty. Even at this time it was felt that some of the higher reaches of the Admiralty did not understand the importance of the striking power of aircraft and regarded them purely as an adjunct to the battleship. They were also extremely jealous of the allocation of manufacturing capacity to Bomber Command and were constantly attempting to divert them towards anti-submarine work.

I enjoyed my time in Bomber Ops. It was very competent with a capacity for getting its own way. Part of the technique was to use one able and much decorated Wing Commander, Joe Collier, to annoy the Admirals. At any committee meeting he could be relied upon to reduce the Naval opposition to a state of apoplexy. This totally destroyed their case, while never giving them any excuse to accuse him of rudeness or disrespect for senior officers.

The Navy at one point put up a scheme for sinking the *Tirpitz* with a device known as the B-bomb. The idea was that you dropped the B-bomb close to the battleship at a certain depth, and a fuse blew the heavy nose cap off and released air into a flotation chamber which brought the bomb up below the battleship and blew a hole in the unprotected bottom. The B-bomb was in fact a piece of theoretical nonsense. When the B-bomb scheme was put to Air Chief Marshal Harris, his reply was short and to the point. 'Tell the Navy they might as well try sinking the *Tirpitz* by stuffing her hawse hole with butter.'

Life in London was not dull. We had the buzz bombs, one of which hit part of the Air Ministry itself beside the Strand. When telephoning this particular branch, if you heard another buzz bomb, you could be sure that your correspondent would say, 'Excuse me. Someone has come into the room.' You could practically hear him getting under the table. I took a flat in Maida Vale at a very cheap rent from a lady who had departed into the country to get away from the buzz bombs. Lindsay came down, against the wishes of her mother and my parents but to my great joy, and we set up house there. I was much amused by some of the arrangements: in the morning, one of us had to stick our head out of the window and coal would be sent up on a lift to be hauled in at our particular stop. As a precaution against the buzz bombs, we turned our bed with the head towards the window. This was quite sensible, as at least it was some protection against flying glass.

Lindsay went back to work in the Ministry of Transport where she was an Assistant Principal and we enjoyed London in wartime in spite of a shortage of food. My mother very kindly sent us a chicken, butter and eggs, but owing to a certain optimism in her packing and a delay in the postal services, they arrived inextricably mixed. Parts of the chicken were still edible.

When the first V2 rocket bomb exploded, I was buying gin which was also in scarce supply. I had to grab the bottle quickly before the assistant serving me dropped it. 'What was that?' he said, and I replied, 'It must have been a gas main.' This was the official explanation until it had to come out that these rockets were the German secret weapon.

In fact the V2 as it manifested itself was not nearly as frightening to Londoners as was the earlier buzz bomb. That could be heard approaching and then the engine cut out. Practically everyone ducked until the noise of the explosion. This made them much more nerve racking than the V2: no one was aware of that until it exploded, so if you were going to be hit, you were dead before you knew it. I came out of the flat one morning and walked along the road towards the tube station to find that a block about 150 yards behind us had been destroyed by a V2 in the night, without disturbing our sleep.

The V2 situation was nonetheless touch and go. It does not bear thinking about what would have happened if the Germans had got an atomic warhead. This was the terror in the minds of the Government. As it was, if Bomber Command had not bombed Peenemunde success-fully, and if the techniques for mass raids had not been evolved, it is probable that the Germans would have had enough V2s to devastate London and indeed any part of the south-east coast they wanted to hit, with grave results for any invasion plans.

While at the Air Ministry I had close contact with a number of Squadrons and I found out that an old friend, Dudley Farmer, was in command of the Second TAF Communications Flight. I rang him up and said, 'Dudley, I have a day off and I want to go over to Normandy to purchase some cheese.' He replied, 'OK I'm going there on Wednesday and you can be my navigator.' I got down to the station in the morning and we took off in an Anson for a newly constructed landing field behind the lines in Normandy. It was rather a pleasant little strip beside an orchard. We went to the mess: the doctor knew all the local farmers and I went with him to see if any Camembert was available. After some confusion about my name which they thought referred to the Maquis (the resistance group), they protested that the Americans had bought all their cheese.

We returned to the airstrip empty-handed. It was a beautiful day and

Dudley and I lay down beside the aircraft and fell asleep. We suddenly heard a great noise, somebody shouting and klaxons going. Down the road came a cavalcade preceded by a jeep with an army officer, shouting, 'Clear the way!' followed by motorcycle outriders and two staff cars, followed by more outriders. Dudley and I looked at each other and he said, 'Ah, we are flying back the Adjutant General. This must be he.' We got up and put our hats on. A very kindly 'old man', Sir Ronald Adam, stepped out of the vehicle. Dudley and I saluted as smartly as we knew how and we chatted for a moment and Dudley said, 'When you are ready, Sir,' and he said, 'When you are ready, my boy,' so we got into the old Anson together with the General, his ADC – a rather pop-eyed young peer – and an airman who was going back on compassionate leave.

We took off and Dudley said to the General, 'We'll fly you over the Mulberry Harbour so you can have a good look.' We flew over it at 1,000 feet but when we were about a mile out to sea, both engines stopped. I looked at Dudley and Dudley looked at me. He pressed the button and the tanks appeared to be full. I snatched a quick look round; the airman was asleep, the General was looking quite calm, and the ADC's eyes were sticking out in great alarm.

The only thing to do was to change the tanks and hope for the best. We did that and the engines came on. We were mighty relieved as the penalty for dropping the Adjutant General in the drink would certainly not have been light. When we got back to Lyneham, Dudley said to the General, 'I hope you did not mind us running the tanks dry, sir, but with all the petrol being run in by the Navy, we like to save every drop.' The General assured him all was well and offered me a lift back to London, which I declined. I asked the ADC if he had been frightened. He said, 'Not at all. Not at all!' I said, 'By God, you looked it.' I went back to London by public transport as I thought we had pushed our luck far enough.

In the summer of 1944 I was called back to Witchford for an Investiture on the aerodrome by the King. All those who had received decorations in the previous year were summoned. There were seventeen in all, of whom seven were pilots. We all assembled in a grand reunion on the night before the ceremony. Group Captain Sim foolishly arranged a rehearsal in the Officers Mess at 7.30 p.m., by which time the party was in full swing and a very unruly and irreverent band of 'heroes' were put through their paces. Next morning we were much more subdued and the hangovers introduced a solemn air, much more suitable for the ceremony. The Queen and the two Princesses were there, and the whole event was a great success and pleased everyone on the Station. Bobby Annan was first up and I was next. The Monarch pinned on my DSO and chatted, but he had been badly briefed and he thought I had just taken over the Squadron. I could see this was a bit awkward so I saluted reasonably smartly and pushed off.

As a Squadron Leader, it was extremely good for me to learn the techniques of staff work. I was particularly fascinated by the way that clever staff officers got their own way. My boss was Wing Commander 'Pete' Tassell, a solicitor in civilian life. He was an administrator, not an operational officer, but understood the business of providing and forecasting bomb requirements. We became good friends. It became obvious that we were to have a shortage of high explosive bombs and that the only capacity available was in the States. When I had done a great deal of work on the shortage, he instructed me to prepare a paper for the Head of Bomber Ops, Air Commodore Sydney Bufton. Pete then went through it carefully and said, 'That is ideal. All the facts are there and you have said "a spate of signals has crossed the Atlantic". Sydney Bufton will read through it, then he will go through it again, he will cross out "a spate" and put in "many" and the rest of the paper will go through to the Chief of Staff unaltered.'

We took it up to him about half past one in the morning and waited while the great man went through the paper. He then read it through again, took out his pen, scored out 'spate' and put in 'many' and okayed the paper. Pete Tassell winked at me over his head and we went home satisfied that we were very clever people.

The staff of Bomber Ops was, I thought, very high quality. Sydney Bufton was one of the ablest of the young Senior Officers, but I suppose the guru there was Group Captain Arthur Morley. A sage-like figure, he had been an Observer in the first war and then was in business in Birmingham, where he made a name for himself in municipal and public work before coming back into the RAF at the outbreak of war. He had a good analytical mind and a great deal of political skill and that essential thing, a knowledge of how people work. He was a brilliant assessor of the successes of different types of operations and was often credited with spotting the fact that the German use of high explosives combined with incendiaries was much more effective than high explosives alone.

One strange importation was John Strachey, the left-wing politician and writer, who had been brought in to put the arguments of the groups into good English and to have a certain political influence. I cannot say that he inspired a particular comradely feeling in me, although at that time I was just recovering from the influence of the Left Book Club.

They were backed up by a very good team of young operational officers, all of whom had had war experience. They needed to be formidable because they were dealing with an extremely tough character in Air Chief Marshal Arthur Harris, with direct access to Churchill. It is always a great irritant to commanders in the field that their general objectives are laid down by a department under the umbrella of the Chief of Air Staff, so the co-operation between the Directorate of Bomber Operations and Bomber Command was an uneasy one.

Harris' toughness was certainly needed in a Commander in Chief at that time and although Bomber Ops was frequently in conflict with Bomber Command, it was the sort of relationship that did produce results. Bomber Command was used pre and post the Normandy invasion to great effect on transport centres. It made a massive contribution to the failure of the Germans to stop the invasion in the first few days as they could not bring their reserves to bear. One could go on forever on the tactics employed, as to whether all efforts should have been concentrated on communications or on fuel, but the fact remains that in the end Bomber Command and the US 8th Air Force were a major factor in winning the war, if not the major factor.

After some nine months in the Air Ministry, I felt that I had been there long enough. Lindsay, to her great joy, had found herself pregnant and departed to Aberdeen to look after her mother who had become ill. I tried to get back on flying, but I was turned down. Thereupon I wrote a quatrain of doggerel about each member of the Directorate starting with the Air Commodore and circulated it. I quote three verses – the first about the much decorated Joe Collier:

> Joe is large and sprayed with gongs
> To B. Ops One this brute belongs.
> He oft is extremely rude
> And would be ruder if he could.

About Hal Lawson, who was in fact a very nice man, I wrote:

Lawson is inclined to pander
Hence his rise to Wing Commander
With senior ranks he is au fait
And gets much more so every day.

About John Strachey, I expanded it to six lines. He was prospective Parliamentary Labour Candidate for Dundee at the time:

Strachey is extremely clever
Living in the Never Never
He writes and talks an awful lot
Dundee should stick to what she's got!
The Socialists' side he has his seat on
And yet his sons will go to Eton.

I followed immediately after this with a request for posting which was granted. I went back up to Scotland to Brackla. It was a relocation unit for aircrews who had done a tour and were being reposted either as instructors or to ground duties. The station was commanded by Group Captain Emmet, a South African, who at the age of 14 had ridden with Rey's Commando in the South African War. He became interested in flying and had come over to Britain for training. When war broke out he joined the Royal Flying Corps. He was just due to retire; I was president of the Mess Committee when he did so and we gave him an epic dinner. He drank, as indeed we all did, an enormous amount and when I met him next morning he was not feeling 100 per cent. I had to smile when he said, 'Mackie – you should not have given me that cigar after dinner!'

I got the job as Commanding Officer of the Officers Squadron, purely because I had done a lot of operations and was large and could look fierce when required. As you can imagine, these young men did not take kindly to hanging about awaiting posting and wanted to go back on flying. Furthermore, they had done a tour and were, of course, somewhat cock-a-hoop. They got into all sorts of scrapes and we had to watch them with care and often rescue them from trouble.

One young man had been caught with aircraft petrol in his car, which was a very common type of ill-doing in the Service. He was court-martialled. I was his defending officer and made a plea not to be too hard on this officer and destroy his career and prospects by a severe reprimand. Thereupon the prosecuting officer leapt to his feet and said, 'Squadron Leader Mackie, do you know that he could go to jail?' I was rather shaken, but countered by citing the young man's operational record, and suggesting that the prosecutor was getting a little excited. Anyhow, the reprimand he got off with was indeed very small.

Brackla was a pleasant station for me. Situated as it was in Morayshire, it adjoined a very good distillery and was near Aberdeen so Lindsay came up quite often. The leisure activities suited me down to the ground; as we could get cartridges for clay pigeon shooting, we became quite popular with the local estates. One estate had a lot of capercaillie; the cocks are the size of a turkey, but with quite a small wing span, and as soon as they got over the edge of the trees, they used to glide. It looked as though this was a peaceful, slow, process, but in fact they were going at an enormous speed in order to make up for the small size of wing. We had a day there shooting: I managed to kill one cleanly, but all the others I missed by a mile because of misjudging the speed.

I also went to a roe deer drive. There were large numbers of roe deer doing a lot of damage to young trees in the area. We were using shotguns with the largest shot we could get and I must say I did not care for shooting these beautiful creatures with a shotgun. I am glad to say that this practice has now stopped.

The powers that be then moved the unit from Brackla down to Catterick. This was a permanent station with a large complement of houses and nearer the centre of things. It was not nearly as good for me, but we had the racecourse next door and many pleasant Yorkshire pubs about. There was a good deal of land on the station and as well as being President of the Mess Committee I became an RAF farmer, cultivating a fair bit of land for potatoes and vegetables and running some sheep. During my stay there, Lindsay, who by this time was heavily pregnant, came down for the weekend after being much distressed because our little spaniel pup had been killed in the street in Aberdeen. There was a race meeting at Catterick and I was rather embarrassed when, referring to a chestnut mare, Lindsay said in a loud voice, 'I like the ginger one.' I remember the ginger one well. It was called Little Pip. Lindsay backed it and so did I. It won at 12-1.

The war in Europe ended on 7 May 1945 and on VE Day Lindsay produced a daughter. We called her Lindsay Felicia in view of the felicitous coincidence of her birth. When I came up to Aberdeen to see my daughter I arrived off the night train and viewed the new arrival in the morning. I thought she looked like other babies, but I spoke words of great appreciation. I then went to a company lunch with my father and did not get away until after 3 o'clock. Mother and baby had been waiting since 2 o'clock and it was a long time before I was forgiven.

I changed jobs and went to Church Fenton – an attractive station and in most enjoyable countryside – on the selection side of the business as against the disciplinary side. We had large numbers of ex POWs coming through who wanted to continue their RAF career and get back to flying. These men were a joy to work with and were of a very high calibre; they were the cream of the ex POWs, and those who had been imprisoned for three or four years were, I must admit, of a great deal higher quality than the average air crew officer by the end of the war.

One very attractive young Australian had an amazing record in the escape committee and went back on flying. Then he was killed in a flying accident that was not in any way his fault. That was a particularly tragic case. Another former POW had been CO of my own training flight at Lossiemouth in 1940. In 1941 he was shot down and taken prisoner. He was still Squadron Leader, but so now was the sprog Pilot Officer he had trained. Unlike me, however, he was a regular officer, went straight back into the Service and finished as an Air Marshal.

I wrote to my father saying that I would be glad if he could be looking for a farm for me. I did not want any of his farms in Aberdeenshire, thinking that the 'deep south' – in other words, Angus or thereby – was the place I would like to farm, in the good land. My father, I understand, was delighted by my letter and said to my mother that the boy was learning sense.

He proceeded with my brother John to look for a farm. There was a rather nice one in Perthshire, near Bridge of Earn, for sale at about £13,000. The father had died and the son was thinking about selling the big farm, paying out his sisters, and taking a small farm himself. My father liked the farm, but he had a strong sense of continuity and asked the young man about his position. He then advised him to keep the farm, and borrow the money to buy out his sisters, saying he would be in a far, far better position than running a small farm. The young man took his advice and may have been grateful to my father for it – but it is unlikely.

There were two farms in Angus: one to rent, the farm of Benshie, or Mains of Ballinshoe, on the Strathmore Estate, and a farm called Meikle Coull for sale, again at about £13,000 for fully 400 acres. We looked at both; Benshie was much the better farm and my father decided, with my total concurrence, that it was the one to go for. My father had an entirely different attitude towards landlords than most farmers and was willing to spend his own money if he was getting a return for it. In the offer for Benshie he said that he would build two cottages on the farm; if the estate would pay for one, he would pay for the other, with no claim on the estate. He also said that he would build at our own expense a potato shed on the farm. He then offered a rent of 36s.6d. an acre for a nineteen year lease and we went down to see the Factor, Gavin Ralston, a very nice man. His father had factored the Strathmore Estates before him.

I was staying with my mother-in-law in Aberdeen and when my father came in to collect me I was wearing my kilt. He looked at me and then he said, 'Go and put on your regimentals. It won't do any harm.' I did what I was told and the first thing Gavin Ralston did was ask me what my medals were, and I have no doubt that this had some effect along with the good rent and the offer to spend money on the place. Anyhow, it was decided to let it to me as against a number of very old established tenants who were offering for the farm.

The land at Benshie was well worth having. It is a medium sandstone loam and has been farmed for a long time. Pat Arnott, the tenant who was giving it up, was a bachelor and a well-known character. He was tenant of the two biggest farms on the Strathmore Estate, Mains of Glamis and Mains of Ballinshoe, as well as having two grazings up the glen. He was very nice to me. It was a pleasure to take over from him and I hope he was pleased by his successor. I told him about my plans to dairy and he allowed me to stay in the house until the sale, looked after by his housekeeper, Mrs Norrie, and her cats, and he gave me a lot of good advice. We were sitting on a seat in front of the house looking over the valley and he said, 'Man, loon, you can farm this place from your bed. It is easy land. The Mains of Glamis is far more difficult and I really have given up the wrong farm.'

He grinned, of course, as he said so. Just after I had told him about my dairying plans, he looked over the valley, pointed to the farm of Mains of Brigton, and said, 'My auld friend, Tam Hay, said to me after the last War, he said, Pat there's ower mony of they sharney-hippit buggers fae the west coming into oor country!' (An expression used of cattle, sharney-hippit means to have a rear smeared with dung.)

I had leave from the RAF to take up the harvest when we got Benshie. But when I went back to Church Fenton and applied for more leave it was refused. I then went to a friend of mine, Kimber, who was by this time in the Postings Branch of the Air Force, and asked him to get me to an airfield near Benshie. He rang me up in some distress and said, 'I can get you to Tealing' (which was only twelve miles from the farm), 'but you will have to drop a rank.' I replied that I would be out in two or three months and that the rank did not matter.

So I got my posting to Tealing, which was the Headquarters of the Radar Group covering Scotland, and I was supposed to be one of the staff. When I informed the Group Captain that I was farming and did not intend to do much work, he looked a little displeased, but I suppose that as he had spent the war on the staff (being a specialist), he thought that this ex-operational chap would only be there for a short time and he would afterwards get someone who did want to work.

So I was once again installed in Benshie and attended my work at Tealing irregularly. On 2 January 1946 I was demobilized. I went up and was measured for my suit and discharged. I met my old friend Maurice Hartford who was flush with money at the time and dined with him in the Savoy. There we had an extremely alcoholic evening. I was put on the train and fell asleep at once and awoke when the train was running into Edinburgh. I must have been fairly cheery before, because when I woke up there were a lot of bright and cheery 'good mornings' from the other occupants of the carriage, and I had no hangover whatsoever.

I felt rather strange, in that the RAF had been my life for the past six years. Excited as I was by my new farm and my first married home, I did feel immensely nostalgic. I have had an extremely interesting time since then, but nothing has ever equalled the pace of life during those six years of war. And perhaps a good thing too.

CHAPTER 9

Benshie

MAINS OF Ballinshoe, or Benshie, as I quickly came to call it, is two miles from Kirriemuir and four miles from Forfar. While many of my RAF comrades were still looking for a job and a home, this was the place I was lucky enough to come to after the War. We had 470 acres of arable and 40 or 50 acres of scrub woodland. On a rise of about 300 feet stood the steading and farmhouse – about a hundred years old, and set overlooking the Howe of Strathmore to the Sidlaw Hills.

It was a very pleasant house, built to a pattern used in the county of Angus with attractive central chimneys, four bedrooms upstairs, one of which had been turned into a bathroom, dining-room and drawing room down below, kitchen and sitting room at the back with two further bedrooms downstairs. One of them was the maid's room, with bars on the window to keep away the lusty young inhabitants of the bothy.

There was an old walled garden, with the shell of a small tower known as Benshie Castle. Opposite this we had the ruins of a little mansion house which had succeeded the castle, and had now been divided into three cottages. The steading had a big barn, a threshing mill engine, stable and cattle courts. Opposite the house, across a small public road, were the shed for five pairs of carts, the old loft, and the cow byre, with the grieve's house and bothy on the end of the range. Its roof was of Glamis slate. It was a very handsome building, which I hope is now listed.

I settled down to farming, and Lindsay settled in with young Lindsay in the house. It was pretty bare. Nevertheless, we were proud and happy in our new home. We had an old black range in the kitchen, flag floors and rats in the house. We had no electricity. Until we got on the grid after about a year, we used Tilly lamps. We made some improvements to the kitchen, taking out the range and putting in a Rayburn cooker before we rose to the giddy heights of an Aga. We had quite a lot of good glass and that sort of thing as wedding presents, but all the furniture had to be bought second hand. I got some at the roup, including the stair carpet, and we went to sales to buy the rest. We got some nice pieces, and we should have bought a lot more at the time. We built a tennis court and opened up the garden. It was so windswept that Lindsay lost heart: the wind normally destroyed any efforts at a flower border. However, we planted shelter trees all around the farm. When they grew quickly and made an enormous difference, she took up gardening again.

To begin with, we got a very nasty blow at the valuations. Valuation was rather a complex business. The valuators looked at the crop in the field and decided how many quarters of grain per acre it would yield (a quarter of oats was 3 cwts; a quarter of barley was 4 cwts). The opposing valuators put their ideas as high or as low for their clients as they could without appearing foolish. The oversman, who was supposed to be independent, then set the rate per acre. The actual value had to await the fiar's prices which were struck annually. The sum was then paid over to the outgoing tenant. My valuator was a friend of my brother John called John Salmon, who was a very shrewd farmer but had just started in the valuation business. Pat Arnott's valuator was Mr Graham, the auctioneer, whom Pat said he was obliged to employ, and the oversman was Mr Fleming, Old Montrose. They got into a horse and cart and trampled over the crops putting a value on each field. When we threshed the crop out, which we did by hired combines, very new at that time, I lost a thousand pounds on the deal. The combines got every ounce of grain and I would have lost much more if we had harvested by binder and threshing mill. I cannot really blame the valuation as the difficulty is well known, but it hurt all the same. A thousand pounds was a lot of money in 1945.

I laid plans to recoup the losses by growing over 200 acres of barley which was the most profitable crop then. As I was still not sure of combine harvesting, I planned to go back to threshing out of the stook and cutting in the conventional way. Sure enough, we grew excellent crops and got them cut with the binder and stooked in reasonable conditions. It then rained for six weeks. We did everything possible – we set up the stooks again, and we built them into little ricks. Eventually, with heavy losses, we got some extremely wet barley into sacks. I was greatly helped by the Angus Milling Company who took the grain to their Glen Coull Mill and dried it. That was, of course, quite expensive. We eventually got the harvest in, but the hoped-for vast profits disappeared into thin air.

We then lifted our potatoes which were a fair crop and went into the winter of 1946/47. At the end of January 1947 came the biggest snowstorm I have ever seen. We were closed in for weeks at a time. We had just started milking and we had to get the milk out, so we broke a route across the fields down to Padanaram where the main road was open. My skis came in extremely handy. We could get a tractor across fields with the milk and never failed to get it away, although sometimes it was two days old. The storm eventually blew itself out, but in April we were still harrowing the snow lying at the dyke sides in order to melt it more quickly.

We got all our barley sown by 20 April. This was followed by one of the best summers we had had for a long time. I went back to combining and we got the whole harvest in, in a fortnight, with both straw and grain in good condition, and I had my cheque within a month. These two years taught me that nothing was certain in farming, except you had to be on your toes.

My plans for dairying were much helped by the fact that my father and two brothers sold me heifers at a very cheap price to give me a start. We made the stable into a milking parlour. The nice old factor insisted that we agree to put the mangers and travises back as they were. This amused me somewhat, as I was sure there would never again be another draught horse on the place. The stable for the farmer's ponies became the dairy and milk room and we kept the cows loose in courts.

When the in-calf heifers were approaching their time and the milking parlour was finished, I started looking for a dairyman. Jim Thomson, an Orkneyman, had been a businessman in London and a member of the London Scottish. He went through the war refusing a commission and finished up as a Regimental Sergeant Major. After the war he wanted back to Orkney, but when he went home, he found that his brother-in-law was really the farmer of the Orkney farm. The North of Scotland College by then had started a dairy cattleman's course; he took it and was the top student. We got on extremely well at the interview and I engaged him as head stockman. The interesting thing was that a very shrewd farmer, Jim Barron of Findowrie, had also looked at him, but he had taken the second student instead because he thought that Jim was so good that either he would take his own farm or move on.

I now had to have somewhere for Jim to live. The accommodation for the men at Benshie at that time was very basic. There were no bathrooms at all. The only decent cottage on the place was the grieve's house and even it had only a tap in the back kitchen. Next door to it was a fairly typical Angus bothy. One of the men was let off early in order to prepare the meal there for the rest of the single men, but how well prepared it was one can imagine. Stories were told about the porridge being made and poured into a drawer and eaten cold. It is said that many of the single men suffered from stomach trouble in later life. The diet was certainly monotonous.

One farmer suspected that his hens were going into the pot for the single men. In the evening, as the boys were just about to begin their tea, he dropped into the bothy, sat down on the stool and proceeded to chat. The chat went on for 25 minutes with the young bothy boys getting more and more impatient. Eventually the foreman seized the pot which was on the traditional swey hanging over the fire, pulled it out and said in a loud, strong voice, 'God knows what will come oot, but it was a rabbit that gid in.'

No doubt they were cheery places, as most places where young men live tend to be, but they were not really very good. The first thing I did was to turn the bothy and grieve's house into a hostel for six men, installing bathrooms, and I engaged a housekeeper to look after them. This was strongly approved of and, as a result, I got a lot of excellent single tractor and dairymen. We put Jim Thomson in one room in the hostel and a tractorman and young dairyman in the other two rooms. It was not luxurious, but it was a big advance on the Angus bothy and, indeed, the average Angus farm cottage.

We also pressed into use what was known as 'the Irishmen's Bothy'. This was as crude a shed as one could wish to see and shows the racist attitude towards the hard-working itinerant Irish labourers who came to work at busy times. We did this shed up, lining it and really making it quite respectable, and we often put students in there.

Jim Thomson set about the dairy with great efficiency. As a former Regimental Sergeant Major, he stood no nonsense from young dairymen and the milking always started on time. I got up at 4 o'clock for the first fortnight, and I am happy to say that, after that, the only time I saw the morning milking was when I came home late.

Jim stayed with me for three years; he not only built up the dairy herd, but also started a small herd of pedigree Wessex pigs. We actually took a first at the Highland Show with a sow – no Mackie had ever won a pedigree prize there before, I think. Jim then bought a farm outside Aberdeen. He became a member of the Aberdeen Milk Market Board and a much-respected member of the farming community. By the time Jim left, we had got a man called Purves in Montrose to build two new houses, in concrete blocks with asbestos roofs. They were well planned but jerrybuilt really. (Later on we spent a good deal of money putting on proper roofs and insulation.) I was therefore able to engage a head dairyman, and give him a good house next door to Fred Kydd, the grieve, who had the other new house.

I cannot say that I ever liked dairying, but it did give a regular income and was more profitable than beef cattle. Once, we had a dance in the potato shed, which we called 'The Tattie Shed Trot'. It was quite a big affair and we did them well as regards food. I told the dairyman to separate enough milk for five gallons of cream, which he did with an ill grace. The dance was a great success and people enjoyed the food and the cream. The next day I went out as was my wont, and one of the first things I did was to go along to the dairy to see how much milk had gone that morning. I looked at the chit and the milk was up five gallons. 'Oh,' I said, 'that was very good,' and suddenly it hit me. I shouted for the dairyman and asked, 'Where the hell did you put the skimmed milk?' He looked at me and said, 'I put it back in the tank.' I said, 'Good God, don't you realise if they had taken a test, I would have been in deep trouble and maybe even in jail?' He looked at me and said, 'They never tak a test on the Sabbath!' It was difficult for me to appear stern, but I did my best.

Starting farming in the area at that time was extremely interesting and also very, very much easier than today. The 1947 Agricultural Act gave guaranteed prices. Although much lower than we would have got on a free market in 1947, there was security because they were guaranteed over a long period. There was also a great feeling of advancement – everyone was relieved that the War was over and new methods were coming in at a tremendous pace. My brother John, who by this time had extensive contacts through his work on mechanisation, used to organise trips in which we would visit the most progressive farmers all over the country. Land was selling then for about £100 an acre, and if we had had the foresight to borrow and buy in large quantities, we would all have become rich.

We were, however, making a good living and food production was rising. We were soon wholly into combining and mechanisation was advancing rapidly. Perhaps the biggest advance came when Harry Ferguson produced his small tractor with hydraulic operation of the plough and other implements.

Grass – its use and preservation – was at the centre of agricultural advance. The old method of haymaking was subject to such variation because of the weather that the artificial drying of grass became a growing sector. If you were in dairying, which gave a sufficient return to pay the extra expense, and because of the very high prices of protein in the form of linseed cake, grass drying was an economic method of producing winter food. At the same time we had the advance in silage-making, which again took much of the risk out of preserving winter keep. We had to learn that while you could make silage with fairly wet grass, the quality was not high and it could deteriorate into almost inedible material, with a most unpleasant smell. I installed a grass drier at Benshie. It was expensive, but nevertheless produced some good winter fodder for the cows.

A friend of mine, Donald Ritchie, thought that he would like to go farming when he came out of the army. He had very little capital, but he came to me as a student. With his agile brain, he learned very quickly. A farm of about 200 acres beside Kirriemuir called Herdhill came on the market in 1947; it had a splendid view over the Howe of Strathmore, lay all to the south and had some very good land on it.

I had another old friend from my rugby playing days – George Raeburn. He went to France with the 51st Highland Division, along with his brother Scott (who was killed before the main battle of France began), and was taken prisoner at St Valery. He spent nearly five years in prison camp where he did a lot of good work on the escape committee and was the officer in charge of the secret communications with the UK. He used to have meetings with the senior officer in charge of the camp in the only private place, which was the loo. He also wrote some excellent articles on prison life and on birds. When released he was promoted and came out on demob as a captain. He went back to his uncle in the family law firm and said, 'Well now, what are my prospects?' His uncle said, 'We need you badly, and in spite of the fact you have not had any experience for the last five years, we will pay you the salary we were paying you when you left.' This salary, I think, was about four pounds per week. George thanked him, and departed to look for something else. He retained his great interest in farming.

The three of us – George Raeburn, Don Ritchie and I – decided that we would have a look at setting up a grass drying unit on this farm at Herdhill. We bought it – borrowing most of the money from the Bank – and went into business. Don got married and moved into the house at Herdhill. We did moderately well in the first year. But by the end of our second it was obvious that the overheads were too high, and that paying a partner a reasonable salary was an expense that this small farm could not bear. George Raeburn advised us to wind it up. But Don, of course, did not want to lose his house and start again.

I then proposed that I would buy the farm and run it in conjunction with Benshie. Don would stay in the house and run a duck-keeping venture. For by then it had struck me that the duck was bound to be a winner: it would eat cheap food, rough draff (brewers grains) and lay far more eggs than the hens did at that time. I myself had looked at various duckeries and settled with the Dutch plan of small straw bedded pens outside and the Khaki Campbell duck. We set them up at Benshie in the old orchard. We had over 2,000 birds there and Andrew Beattie, who lived with his parents in one of the old houses down past the orchard, had been put in charge with a pony and cart and egg washing machines.

George Raeburn, who was very much shrewder, said that rather than go into duck-keeping by himself, Don should give up farming and get a job there and then. But he agreed to the plan as it would let him out of his obligation. What I should have done in fact was kept Herdhill and farmed it tightly along with Benshie, and Don should have taken George's advice and got a job immediately.

But I bought the farm and we went ahead. After a year or so I was still heavily borrowed and I decided that I should sell it. So that Don could have the house and space for his ducks, I bought another 200-acre farm, Cantsmill. This cost me £6,000. I then put Herdhill up for auction and it made £15,000, which was a happy acquisition of capital for me.

My own ducks did all they were supposed to do. They laid something like 300 eggs a year. Feeding them on a mixture of blood meal and draff was extremely profitable – until some silly ass died from salmonella got from a duck's egg. The price halved overnight. It did not recover and my duck enterprise had to come to a stop. Don too was hit by the fall in the price of the eggs. He gave it up and took a job with S.A.I. where he did very well until he retired. Although because of the rising price of land, I got out without loss, this venture in grass drying and ducks was one of great enthusiasm and bad judgment.

As I got busier, I appointed Captain Aithie as my secretary – an ex quartermaster, a large man who had been for many years in the army and was eventually commissioned. If I wanted to see a man, Captain Athie would roar at him in the manner of a sergeant major bringing a defaulter before the commanding officer. Nevertheless, the men tolerated him and indeed liked him – they found it amusing more than anything else. We also had a young girl from Forfar as his assistant until I saw a diseased cat outside the office. I grabbed my gun and shot it. The poor girl had to be taken home in hysterics and never came back.

We added to the house years later in 1964, putting a storey on to the back wing to give us five bedrooms upstairs. Although I did not install central heating, which was probably a mistake, I think we made rather a good job of it: we lifted the roof, putting back the old slates, and put the same windows above as below, so that most people thought that it was the original. We made a large room down below with a big fire, which acted as both a living room and hall. It still left a slight awkwardness in getting through the kitchen, but on the whole it worked well.

At the same time we did up the new cottages, which had been fairly austerely built just after the war and put a new roof on to the old cottages down beside the castle. When the single men got married and moved out to newly-built council houses nearby, we turned the hostel back into two cottages.

I dairied for 25 years before – with a sigh of relief – dispersing the herd for very good prices in 1970. I went into the rearing of calves instead, making up the income by going in for soft fruit, mainly strawberries, in a larger way than previously. We went in for calf rearing on a big scale, overseen by an admirable stockman called Peter Caul. One year, he raised 500 calves and lost only four. I may say it was not rewarded by the prices that we received, and I think he nearly killed himself doing it. But it was a terrific feat.

Although I do remember one or two bad years, the farm in those days, particularly in dairying, made money really quite easily. Certainly, we lived extraordinarily well and happily. My daughters Lindsay and Diana were born within two years of each other. This turned out to be an excellent thing as we had an incompatibility in our blood groups. I was double positive rhesus whereas Lindsay was double negative, with the result that our third child, a boy, was born in good health, weighing about eight pounds, but the blood deteriorated and he died. This was a great blow, to Lindsay particularly, and after much trouble, we achieved Jeannie five years later. She was wholly transfused at birth and lived to tell the tale.

The two eldest girls went to Reform Street School in Kirriemuir and afterwards on to Forfar Academy. At 11 or 12, they went on to St Leonards in St Andrews – a very good academic school with a strong 'suffragette' belief that girls should be educated. Jeannie, having had all her blood changed at birth, we did not think would do particularly well at Reform Street, and she went to an excellent little Dame School in Kirriemuir, run by an admirable teacher called Miss Nixon who brought her on extremely fast. The concentration was such, however, that we thought she ought to go to a slightly less academically forced atmosphere and sent her to a private school in Broughty Ferry (of which I was rather ashamed), until she too went to St Leonards.

As the girls were all reasonably academic, we had little trouble with their education. Lindsay and Di both went on to Edinburgh, Lindsay to University and Di to Art College. Di found a flat for them in Whitehorse Close on the Royal Mile, which they occupied with two other girls, and had a small mini van ex my butcher's shop which they used. Jeannie went to St Leonards younger than the others and I think was there too long. Her mother thought quite rightly that we ought to move her and with the co-operation of the excellent Head Mistress, Miss Macaulay, we got her into a Sixth Form College in Suffolk, which she greatly enjoyed. She went on thereafter to do an English degree at Cambridge.

Benshie was really an admirable place to bring up children, and living on the farm was good for them, even if their vocabulary contained a number of words that their mother did not like to hear. With our young daughters growing up, life was good.

CHAPTER 10

Farming in Angus

CTESIPHON SHEDS were the invention of a certain Major Waller. When in Baghdad during the War he was much taken by the fact that the Ctesiphon arch was still standing after 2,000 years. As an engineer, he realised that it was a catenary, shaped like a chain hung between your two hands. Turned upside down as it was, this formed the perfectly stressed Ctesiphon arch. Using this principle, he evolved a method of building sheds with reinforced concrete after the War when materials were extremely short. I simplified his process and built in sections. I made a frame on wheels, 24' wide and 8' across, covered with galvanised sheeting on which we laid sacking. We then laid a 6" layer of concrete with pig wire netting as reinforcing on top of this, along with one or two reinforcing rods, and waited a night. In the morning, when the concrete had dried, we lowered the section and rolled it forward to repeat the process. I put up a potato shed like this which was much cheaper than any other method. However, in the end of the day, I was to bitterly regret using the system.

Jim Robbie was a tractorman I employed. He was a good looking young fellow and very bright. He had a capacity for mental arithmetic that argued a good mathematical brain. He also had a nice dry wit. I got a present of a barrel of beer once and kept it in the office where I dispensed it when I thought it deserved. Jim got a pint on one occasion. 'Normally a tractorman goes to the office to get the sack,' he said. 'But a pint is better.'

His father had been grieve at one or two large farms in the county and he came to me too as an orraman – an all rounder, who could drive a pair of horses, build a stack and sort cattle, and was a very valuable member of the team. Mrs Robbie was a tremendous character who could be very funny. She loved working outside and, I suspect, disliked housework. When in the house she always went about in her bare feet.

Lindsay had a young nursemaid/nanny called Edith McBain. She was immediately targeted by the young men on the farm but Jim Robbie found favour. On Thursday nights Jim came over. He came into the nursery which Edie had all prepared, with an admirable tray all laid, and they spent the evening there in great respectability. Eventually they married and Jim left the hostel to take a married man's job at Mains of Drumkilbo.

A year or so later I decided to change my grieve. Fred Kydd was highly intelligent and able, but I decided that he was not tough enough on the young men. This was probably a mistake: Fred was immediately employed by David Lubbock and went to Mains of Farnell. But I advertised for a new grieve and received a letter which simply said: 'Dear Sir I wish to apply for the job. Yours, J. Robbie.' J. Robbie came back to Benshie. I said to his father, 'How will you like the new grieve?'

He looked at me sideways and said, 'I dinna ken, but I will put up wi' him for a while.'

Jim and Edie settled down in one of the new houses and they had Jimmy and later Angus. Jim Robbie made an admirable grieve and young Jimmy used to wander about following his father at the age of two or three, with his hands in his pockets in the same style, a very hardy, happy young boy.

I decided to knock down one of my Ctesiphon sheds to make room for a better building. The men were demolishing it during a slack period. One section was ready to fall down and Jim stepped back behind the next section. It also collapsed, pinning him against the wall of the next shed. It was an appalling tragedy and young Jimmy saw it happen. Jim died on his way to hospital. After the ambulance left, what particularly sticks in my mind is Edie going down the road back to her house. She was walking like a dazed old woman.

Gloom descended on the whole farm. I blamed myself in that, knowing what I know now, I should never have allowed farm staff to undertake demolition work. Edie was struck all of a heap. She also resented having to move from the grieve's house into a small house down by the castle. But as time went on, she improved. We got Edie to come back to do daily work in the house which aided, I think, in restoring her to normality and certainly was a great help to us. Edie suffered greatly from arthritis of the hip, but after two operations her life changed and she was again in good health. When I retired she bought a house in Kirrie and is there now. She still knits socks for me, to my great delight.

I think that young Jimmy, however, never really recovered from the experience. Although he grew up into an able boy who became a very good mechanic, he had a nervous stomach complaint which never cured. It was responsible, I think for his early death, leaving a widow and three children.

Angus, the baby, was, however, a different story. He was bright like his father and brother and went to University. After graduating he went off to be a town planner. But he disliked it so much that he was actually feeling unwell. He came back to Benshie to drive a tractor. He was extremely happy so doing, and got married. I made him my head fruitman. He handled 50 acres of strawberries, dealing with up to 300 pickers with enormous success. When I eventually came out of the farm, it was he who was in reality the one managing the whole operation for my successor.

In Angus, there was a very lively atmosphere post war with young people coming back from the Forces. With our circle of friends, life was interesting and pleasant. We happily had plenty of help and a nanny for the children. Farming was prosperous and we took full advantage of it to enjoy our young married life. Perhaps our closest friends were the Townleys, Humphrey being an ex-serviceman who rented a farm after the war from his aunt on the Idvies Estate. I was at the butcher's owned by Mr Kinloch in Kirriemuir, a nice, chatty man, when he also introduced me to a tall, brisk young man who came into the shop. This was Angus Patullo. He was from a farming family and, like me, not long out of the forces. He had won a Military Cross at Wadi Akarit. We too became good friends. Like me, he had daughters and no son.

We had good neighbours – another Patullo next door, the Mitchells at Haughs of Benshie, the Bishops at Fletcherfield – two bachelor brothers, later succeeded by a niece, Mrs Mackay, and her sons, and Geordie Maxwell at Ballindarg, who was a potato merchant and a great character in the district.

In 1952 Andrew Lane, who was the brother of a friend of ours, Margaret Thorpe, bought a big house in Dundee in the Perth Road and turned it into a hotel. Andrew and Jacqui, his new French bride, turned the Invercarse into the first really good restaurant in Dundee and it was an immense success. We greatly enjoyed going there and our friendship with Andrew and Jacqui, although they were ten years younger than us oldies.

I had a number of dashing cars. I came out of the Air Force with an Alvis Speed 20 Tourer. But the best one was a 4$^{1}/_{4}$ litre Bentley, which had been converted into a shooting brake. If I had kept them they would have been worth a mint of money. In 1950 we took my then new car, a Humber Super Snipe, to France on our first holiday abroad. We had at that time a foreign exchange allowance of about £300. I do not think up to then I had ever spent more than £50 on a holiday and did not quite appreciate that this allowance, which I was throwing about like a drunken sailor, was my own money. However, we enjoyed it. It was Lindsay's first time abroad and just after getting off the boat at Calais we stopped at a level crossing. A car in front of us suddenly erupted and about five young men strode over to the side and proceeded to relieve themselves in full back view. Lindsay's face was a study. I soon became very practical over vehicles and had a series of large Fords – very useful farmers' cars. Our second car was a little Austin truck, also very useful.

In the early 50s, I said to Lindsay, 'I am going to get you a properly trained gardener.' She readily agreed that in order to pay his wages we would also have to have a few acres of commercial fruit. Bob Spalding was an excellent young gardener, properly trained, who had served his apprenticeship at Fettercairn House. He had been an armourer in the RAF during the war, spending much of his service on bomb disposal. At the end of the first year, Lindsay complained that, apart from odd days, the 'few acres of fruit' were taking up all the attention. However, she went on with Bob to develop a very pleasant garden.

The nearby small estate of Logie was bought by Lord Douglas Gordon, a brother of the Marquis of Huntly, and his nice wife Suzanne. I rented land from him and worked it from Benshie. He went into intensive growing of daffodils under glass. I purchased the spent daffodils at a very low price and Bob Spalding planted them up and down the roadside leading up to Benshie. Before long people used to come in their cars to see the daffodils in bloom. I am happy to say that I was followed by others and a lot of people now have a good show of daffodils along their roadside in spring.

Bob left for the head gardener's job to Sir James Cayzer at one point. But after a couple of years he came back and stayed until he retired, being manager for the last five years. Bob and I got on very well. He drove me about on my various political journeys and, although a Conservative himself, put up with my strange Liberal views. His opinions and mine were in fact practically identical and he certainly was not on the Thatcherite wing of the Conservative Party.

We had a common interest in the RAF and an even more common

one in getting as much out of an acre of strawberries as possible. It depended very largely on the use of herbicides and fungicides and got rather overdone. This was brought home to me when in the field behind the steading we were able to keep strawberries going for up to five or six years fruiting. When, however, we came to plough the strawberries down, we found that no gulls followed the plough, for the earthworms had disappeared.

This shook me. On examining our yields, we also found that although we could crop strawberries for a long time, their quality and size suffered badly. We then went on to a system of two cropping years, i.e. plant one year and pull the flowers off, crop for two years and plough down. We also became much more selective about fungicides and herbicides. The technique improved so that we could keep the berries clean with far smaller quantities of chemicals. Bob kept smack up to date, as with his high intelligence he could follow the new techniques properly. The earthworms survived and multiplied.

Bob's family were all extremely bright and his eldest son, George, is now a mathematician of some distinction working at Harwell. His second son Bobby is a mathematics master in Edinburgh. The youngest son, Billy, did not apply himself to his books, although equally bright, and is now a highly-skilled welder. His daughter Anne is, happily for Bob, married in nearby Forfar and enjoys a good relationship with her father. When Bob retired he bought a house in the Northmuir of Kirriemuir, adjacent to the Golf Course, and occupied himself happily with his golf and other interests.

Although this was traditionally raspberry country, I found that on the whole we could make a better job of the strawberry. The marketing of fresh raspberries had been ruined by the scarcity of raspberries during the war, the growers finding it much easier to pick for pulp which was made into jam. The canners and pulpers were paying good prices. The result was that the more difficult marketing, packaging and picking of quality fruit had been entirely neglected. The pickers preferred raspberries because they didn't have to bend, but we got plenty of strawberry pickers when they found they could make more money.

Along with one or two friends I organised a meeting in the form of a dinner in the Royal Hotel in Forfar in 1959 and we set up a marketing co-operative. We organised the sending, by lorry and train, of raspberries and strawberries to the south and London. We initially had a collection point at Benshie and the first year was very successful, not so much for the quantity of fruit we sold, but in the fact that the canners immediately raised their prices to compete with this new organisation.

We went on to organise a special train from Dundee to London with the fruit the next year and this carried on for a year or two. We acquired premises in Forfar and made a very reasonable impact on prices while at the same time re-establishing fresh Scottish fruit in the taste of the English public. Our great mistake, although we were reasonably successful to start with, was that we did not make it a closed business. In other words, members should have had to market all their own fruit through the co-op and we should have done a great deal more work in sales promotion and research into packaging.

A co-op begun along these lines in North Angus and Mearns is a very successful affair while Perth and Angus Fruit Growers went into liquidation in the late 1990s. Nevertheless, it did a good deal for the small grower.

Shortly after we came to Benshie we started having a bonfire on Guy Fawkes night. Children on the farm collected firewood. The grieve then supervised the construction of a massive fire, hearted with bales of straw and built around with useless bits of wood, old fencing posts, and discarded tree branches. We had a Guy on top and the whole thing was soused in waste oil or diesel. I provided the fireworks; I obtained a lot of fireworks for £5 in the 1940s and 50s and finished years later by spending £30 to get fewer! We put up launching racks for the rockets and we distributed sparklers. The children sometimes provided their own fireworks, while hot chocolate and bridies were contributed by everyone on the farm. At the appropriate moment, I would shout, 'What shall we do with the Guy?' and on the command 'Burn him!', we lit the bonfire.

The straw and oil went up in a very satisfactory manner. Long after the fireworks were finished we stood about chatting round the blaze. Some children have said that they remember this as a great event in the winter season. I must say that my own most enjoyable remembrance was when someone dropped a sparkler into the fireworks box. The whole thing blew up with an astonishing series of explosions which scattered everyone. There were fewer rockets as a result but it was a good talking point. My successor at Benshie has not continued the bonfire – how can he when there is only one family left on the place?

CHAPTER 11

Braeroy

IN 1953 I saw an advertisement for a West Highland Estate near Fort William in Inverness-shire called Braeroy. It had 20,000 acres of ground with three hirsels of black faced ewes and 1,500 wethers up to three years old on the rest of the ground. It had a deer forest as well. Although what I should have done financially was to stick to farming my good low ground, the idea of hill farming and stalking appealed.

I went over to Braeroy and looked at the lodge and was wholly captivated. I met the owner in the Balavil Arms Hotel, Newtonmore, and we struck a bargain at £29,000. I had an overdraft on Benshie, and would have to borrow all the money. My banker in Forfar said in a despairing voice, 'You will have to go to Glasgow.' In Glasgow itself, the Assistant General Manager of the Clydesdale Bank was a large chap with curling eyebrows and a cold, grey eye. His first words were, 'Well, Mr Mackie, this is a great deal of our money you want.'

It was indeed a great deal – nearly £1 million in today's money. I plunged into my tale, explaining how the two farms would tie in, how I would be doing something for the Highlands, how cattle would improve the low ground and keep people in the hills, and how we could market the venison. As I spoke his eye grew colder and colder, but I ploughed bravely on and finished with a peroration about improving the fertility. He looked at me for a moment, and then he sighed, and said, 'It is wonderful. It is what I would like to do myself. Of course you can have the money.'

I found at Braeroy a large and handsome lodge and three or four cottages, a gun room and a deer larder, but, apart from the sheep fanks, no significant farm buildings. When I arrived, I set off with a friend and the head shepherd to have a really good look at the estate. Braeroy lies at the top of Glen Roy, the River Roy running down to join the Spean at Roy Bridge about 11 miles down from the lodge. It was three or four miles up to the top of the property at the White Falls. The land started at 1,000 feet and went up to just under 4,000 feet. We took the jeep up the Glen, and climbed as high as 3,000 feet. Glen Roy is noted for its parallel roads, which are the banks at different levels of a lake in the last Ice Age. The main glen ran up the centre and a subsidiary one ran to the west. Typically West Highland, the acreage could only support the sheep stock and the very large numbers of hinds which wintered on Braeroy.

We had a long and, for me, fairly arduous day. When we got back to the lodge I said to the head shepherd, 'Dochy, you will have a dram?' 'Well,' he said, 'the wife will have the tea ready, but if you insist.' I opened a bottle and we had a dram which we all three greatly enjoyed and then we had another dram which was even more enjoyable, and then, of course, we had to finish the bottle. As Dochy raised his glass for the last time he said, 'Good health and thank God I am not a woman. I would not have been a nice one – I can never say no!'

The lodge itself had large rooms and eight bedrooms. I had made a bargain with the previous owner that he would only remove from the lodge the personal and precious. He interpreted this in a fairly liberal manner, in that he removed most of the bedding and many of the plants, including gentians from the garden. The cooking equipment was antiquated, but it was a pleasant house. We reckoned to go up there for at least six weeks in summer and autumn and the children enjoyed it enormously. I cannot say, however, that Lindsay altogether appreciated the departure from Benshie, where we had excellent help, to this large lodge, where we had some very strange help indeed and visitors all summer.

Perhaps the most interesting of those were Aneurin Bevan and his wife, Jenny Lee, who were great friends of my brother John. We took them far up the glen in the jeep and they greatly enjoyed it. In the evening after dinner we started talking politics. With impeccable logic, I drove the great man into a corner, and thought I was a very clever fellow. He escaped with ease and finished the argument, to the laughter of everyone else, by saying with great good cheer, 'George, you are a standard bearer without a bloody standard, man!' He disposed of both me and the Liberal Party in one phrase.

We engaged a young stalker called Macgregor, the son of a gamekeeper on the royal estate at Balmoral. His father had made him serve his apprenticeship as a joiner. He then immediately applied for a job as a stalker, so obviously the love of the hills was bred in his bones.

I am unlikely to forget the first stalk that I did with Macgregor. My friend Humphrey Townley was staying. The two ponies, Fly and

Suttie, were lined up, with Molloy as ponyman, and off we set. The first stalk was aborted as often happens – the stag wisely moves off – but on the second Humphrey got a stag. After lunch we went higher up and came into a stag at very short range, which I got. We then had to get the ponies up to the point, drag the stags round to where the ponies could meet them, and walk back to the lodge. Humphrey and I were very tired and our young stalker was not yet as fit as he would later become, though he tried not to show it. We did in the region of twenty miles that day. It was very good for my weight and did my appetite no harm.

I liked stalking, provided I killed the beast cleanly. There was no trouble in getting our regular forty stags off the forest and we were able to let an odd stag to a nearby hotel, which brought in a little income, as well as there being plenty of sport and exercise for ourselves and our friends. The work in hind shooting during the winter was fairly laborious: we used to take about 200. The price of venison at that time was just starting to rise owing to German interest, but it was not a very large proportion of the total income. At that time the market for venison was just opening up and I had the idea that we could sell it in our shop in Dundee. However, excellent prices then became available in Germany for quite a long time.

There were grouse, but like all West Highland estates, the number had decreased enormously during the post-War years. This I thought was due to two main factors. The first, undoubtedly, was the hoodie crow. I sat one afternoon with a set of binoculars, watching a pair of hoodies quartering a hillside in front of me. They were efficient hunters. They were most methodical and swooped on what must have been a number of nests. We did our best to keep them down, but it was very difficult with the large forestry plantations nearby. The second factor was over-grazing by deer and sheep which reduced the amount of heather, compounded by a lack of consistent burning. Our excellent neighbour, Kenny Kennedy, provided an illustration of over-grazing, or what grazing-for-profit would do. On the Braeroy side of the fence it was heather, on the other side it was grass. This was because Kenny kept a flock of the maximum number possible. An extremely able young man, he lived down the glen, but handled his stock of ewes himself on about 2,000 acres. His sheep were good and it afforded him a living.

It was an extraordinary place for children. I took young Lindsay for a walk on the tops of hills a couple of miles from the house and, as we walked along the rigging, out of a den a yard in front of us sprang a dog fox. I was amazed and I had the wit to look down at Lindsay's face and the succeeding emotions passing over were absolutely fascinating. When we got back down, her sister Diana was of course enormously jealous. The next day I had to take her to a natural bridge over another ravine, where I assured her Lindsay had not been. Just 150 yards from our house there was a steep and dangerous ravine with wet rocks. We warned Lindsay and Diana, then aged eight and seven, that on no account were they to go near this ravine. Needless to say, on the second day they were missing, and we found them standing on the bridge pondering what they would do to get down to the water. We were horrified. We marched them back to the house. They must be taught a lesson and I would, for the first time, beat them with a slipper. Fortunately, after the first stroke the slipper flew out of my hand and landed below the sofa. But the threat sunk in and they did not go back alone.

All up and down the Roy there were wonderful pools in which you could bathe. They did not appear then to be as cold as they seem now. I remember a particularly happy day when Ben Coutts and his family came over. It had been warm for a while, so the water was splendid. The children spent practically the whole day in the river. It is true that when you get a really good day in the West Highlands, it is very difficult to imagine anything that can compare with it.

In 1933 the British Aluminium Company built the first hydro-electric dam on the Spean and bought out the fishing on the tributaries. I rented the Roy for £70 a year and, apart from a few people who bought tickets, we fished the whole river. Although a number of my expert friends came over, they had a total lack of success until Alistair Forbes, a friend of my brother's, took one look, and said, 'George, this is a West Highland spate river. It is at the moment falling. I have a bottle of prawns and tomorrow we will spin a prawn.' The next day he and I went out and fished down the river. I caught eight and he caught seven. After this I thought salmon fishing easy and really never attempted fly-fishing, to the disgust of my conservative friends.

There was also great fun to be had in the high lochs and in the burns where a carefully dropped worm or fly running over the edge into a pool would nearly always catch the biggest fish in the pool. There was a loch away at the top of the property, with a five mile walk to it, where anything thrown in the water would take small trout at about three or four to the pound, and we often came back with a basket of these, which were really quite delicious.

And seeing children catching a fish for the first time is a wonderful experience.

The pattern of work in the West Highlands was quite different to the East. They would work extremely hard at the essential times – gathering, clipping and lambing – but did not see the necessity for over exertion at other periods, and the soft air of the glen made them walk happily past a dead sheep for weeks, and never think of taking a spade to bury it. There were exceptions, but in the main, I preferred the robust attitude of the East Coaster.

As I was a lowland farmer in an area where there was plenty of straw and other food, it appeared to me that we should improve the small fields we had at Braeroy, by re-seeding and manuring, and also improve the valley bottoms by putting on up to a hundred cows and feeding them in the winter with concentrates which they got to supplement the roughage left over from the summer season, and thus improve the grazing for the sheep. I cast around amongst my knowledgeable friends and eventually decided to buy Irish black heifers with white faces. We also bought a number of cross Highlanders. The system worked well – we did improve the grazing and our calves steadily made more money at the autumn sales.

One year I found that the bull we had for the job would not serve a cow. My friend Jim Findlay, at that time of the Hatton of Newtyle, said, 'George, I have a big able bull roaming the fences looking for work. You can have him to serve your cows.'

With unusual good sense, I insured the bull, which was a good one. We took it up to Braeroy where we had a cow on heat in the little park beside the lodge. He immediately served the cow. But the very next morning, when we went to take him up to the main herd, we found that he had broken the fence and gone to the hills. I had to report him to the insurance company as lost. A nicely dressed man appeared at the lodge and announced that he was there to check on the disappearance of the bull. I put him in the jeep and drove him up the glen, waved my hand and said, 'Look where you will,' showed him the new bull we had bought and the cows, and he departed, if not satisfied, at least assured he was not fit to find the bull. Jim was paid the insurance money, and six months later we found the bull at the bottom of a deep corrie. He had strayed over it and broken his neck.

We tried to improve the Blackfaced stock. On hill farms many flocks have been on the same area for many generations and have acquired characteristics which are valuable! They are tied to their area and because of this are worth more money. We bought good tups and culled vigorously and kept up the quality. I was also greatly taken with the idea of the three year old wether, who literally needed no looking after, yielding a heavy fleece, which at that time commanded a reasonable price. What I did not realise was that there were occasions when you had heavy losses, which made the wether business variable.

I was eventually very fortunate in getting a really first class head shepherd, who was originally East Coast and insisted on everything being done properly. I had a plan that we would save on shepherds' wages by doubling up, and I explained all this with great care to him. He said he entirely disapproved and if the job was worth doing, it was worth doing well and he personally could not stay on a place where the sheep were not looked after. Economically, of course, I was right, but morally, socially and in every other way, he was right. The extensive system of hill sheep farming, letting the ewes lamb themselves, bearing several losses but saving large amounts of wages is, without doubt, more profitable, but certainly the philosophy of saving ewes and lambs is much more attractive. I caved in at once and he stayed happily with us for a number of years.

At that time I was very keen on the Roadnight system of keeping pigs outside and thought that it would be a very useful addition to income at Braeroy. It worked very well in summer, except that the difficulties of rounding up the pigs were considerable, as they did not react like sheep to a collie dog, and in the winter it was not possible.

I suppose that the only really commercially successful thing we did was the introduction of breeding cows. It certainly improved the grazing in the bottom parts of the Glen and quite improved the quality of the sheep there. I was greatly helped by my old friend Ben Coutts, who was a genuine expert on hill farming and was at the time farming on his own account over the hill at Newtonmore. He and I later formed a company and did quite a bit of work advising estate owners on reducing their losses by better farming. Unfortunately, in nearly every case our advice was not taken, because it would have involved getting rid of incompetent or dishonest employees who had placed their employers under some form of obligation which prevented their dismissal.

After a year, I looked at my investment in Braeroy and found that with cows and other developments, I had nearly doubled the amount of money in the estate. Not being altogether stupid, I saw that my investment was too big, so I cast around for a partner. I was very fortunate that Michael Crichton-Stewart of Falkland Palace was looking for an investment. We met, inspected Braeroy and each other, and produced a rather decent working arrangement. He bought the heritable and rented it to Braeroy Limited, in which we were equal partners, and we arranged that any capital appreciation would be divided between us. I enjoyed our association and so, I hope, did he.

My banker at the time knew nothing of these negotiations. With the cheque in my pocket I went into the bank, and he went into his spiel about the generosity of the bank and my extravagance. I let him run and then said, 'You're right, I'll cut the overdraft by 75 per cent.' He gaped at the cheque, and his jaw hit the table when he realised how much interest he was losing. He was the only Clydesdale Bank manager in Forfar whom I disliked. As long as I told them what I was up to, all the others put up with me in good humour.

I came into the farmyard at quarter to seven one morning to find my bank manager (one of the nice ones) sitting in his car. I said, 'My God, things must be bad!' He grinned sheepishly and said, 'They are. The boy on the cash is £100 short and the inspectors are due – will you please count the wages you drew yesterday?' We opened the safe and we had the extra £100. This particular clerk had made previous mistakes and the manager would have taken the blame.

The whole glen was a typical Highland scenario as it has developed since the break up of the clan system. Braeroy, right at the top, was a sporting estate with a background of sheep farming. Its typical Edwardian lodge could never have been supported in its heyday without being subsidised by a rich man. Right next to Braeroy on the east side of the river was Kenny Kennedy's sheep farm. The next estate down was a club farm with a number of crofters participating in its running. On the other side of the river there was another club farm and at the bottom, another sporting estate.

The club farm at Bohuntine was the one I knew best, as one of the crofters, Dochy McDonald, was head shepherd on Braeroy and another of our shepherds was the son of the leading man on the club farm, Angus Campbell. Angus was a very able West Highlander, with the virtues and the faults of the West. He was clever with his tongue, and I imagine a cleverer man than his brother, who had become the Roman Catholic Archbishop of Glasgow, while Angus stayed behind to take over the family croft and his responsibilities in the club farm.

My brother John, who was on the board of the National Institute of Agricultural Engineering, brought his Directors to Glen Roy on their annual summer tour to the Highlands to look at traditional sheep farming systems. It was a beautiful day and as I led the convoy of cars up the glen, it never looked better. We stopped by the roadside where we were met by Angus Campbell and Mr McGregor of the club. I had, of course, a couple of bottles of whisky in the back and we stood in the glorious sunshine, chatting and having a dram, for some time. The distinguished directors of the NIAE much enjoyed their day, but whether they felt they had a big function in the Highlands, I rather doubt.

Eventually I said to Angus, 'Perhaps Mr McGregor could now explain the financial system.' Mr McGregor said, 'Oh yes, indeed. We get the money in for the wool and then we get the money for the lambs and when we have got the money for the cast ewes, we pay the bills and divide what is left.'

Everybody agreed that in its simplicity this system was positively sublime. But nothing was put to reserve. All was returned to the members, who either saved it or spent it – mostly I think, spent it. This was the root cause of the decline in this sort of share farming, which socially is quite excellent.

Angus Campbell's son Ronnie was the sort of chap who drove me to absolute fury if we went up the hill together, for he would have his hands in his pockets whistling going up a one in five slope, while I was dragging my 18 stone up with many a grunt! We used to hold parties at Braeroy to which we asked our neighbours. They were always great fun in that, after the food, they took the form of a ceilidh. Everyone performed in some way. Ronnie Campbell sang, and sang very well. My wife turned to Angus who was sitting beside her and said, 'You must be very proud of Ronnie, Mr Campbell.' He replied, 'Mistress Mackie, you should not have favourites in your family, but I must admit that that boy Ronnie is the star of my heart.'

The Church of Scotland minister in the district was Doctor Mackinnon, a character, scholar and a man of impressive personality. He was quickly in touch with me to ensure that transport would be provided for people coming to Church and for the general spiritual welfare of any employees. One Easter Sunday we were to Church with a whole host of holiday makers, and a little child was making a noise. Dr Mackinnon suddenly stopped his sermon, and addressed the congregation thus: 'A little child is prattling. Some of you are embarrassed. Do not be embarrassed. It is wholly delightful.'

There was also a pre-Reformation Catholic community in the Parish of Kilmonevaig, headed by Father Dominic Mackillaig. He was a different character, but just as impressive in his way. We had a dram together once at the Lochaber Show and I told him the old but good story of the Catholic priest and the Church of Scotland minister. The minister went to the priest and said, 'We have been quarrelling for years. It is quite wrong. We must be friends, for after all, we both serve the same master.' The priest seized his hand, shook it warmly and said, 'Yes, we both serve the same master. You in your way and I in his!' Dominic laughed heartily, then he turned to me and he said, 'Mr Mackie, you are not a nice man. You put the wit in the voice of the Catholic, but you put the grace of God in the Church of Scotland.'

During the ten years we had Braeroy I greatly enjoyed it and so I think did Michael Crichton-Stewart. But when I got deeply involved in politics it was obvious that I could not spend much time at Braeroy. We put the estate up for sale and eventually agreed with a man called Tapp, from one of the lowest lying pieces of Essex, to sell at a price that did not make us much profit, but did not involve us in heavy loss. I do not really know why Tapp wanted to go to the Highlands with its over 100 inches of rain a year – perhaps he thought it would be a useful refuge against nuclear war.

I remember saying to him, 'You can have the furniture in the lodge and any Old Masters you may find for £1,000.' He stayed a night at Benshie during the negotiations, and saw some pictures of our family painted by William Cadenhead. He liked them and said, 'Do you think he would paint my children?' As Bill was at that time a young struggling artist, I replied, 'Will a duck swim?' Bill was duly engaged to come and paint the Tapp children. He looked round the lodge and said to Tapp, 'I see you have two Samuel Palmers here.' 'Yes, of course,' said Tapp in a rather strange voice. He sold the two pictures for about £3,000. When I heard this, I wrote congratulating him but saying that he might have sent me a bottle of whisky. He replied in the negative.

CHAPTER 12

South Angus and Money Raising

I VOTED LIBERAL IN 1945 for a friend of mine, Ivor Davies, in West Aberdeenshire. I joined the Liberal Party in 1949. Young John Jenkins was our candidate in South Angus in 1950. Educated at Winchester, he was a farmer from Dumfriesshire. He and I became firm friends. We travelled round the glens and villages giving, of course, the same speeches, slightly varied, and we had an exhilarating rally in Arbroath. There were three candidates, Labour, Liberal and National Liberal (Tory), but the Tories with their excellent organisation again went romping home. We came third and listening to the wireless giving out the results, we were pretty devastated. There was a repeated refrain: 'The Liberal and Communist candidates lose their deposits.' This phrase did much to destroy any renewed impetus of Liberalism. We were left licking our wounds.

However, my friendship with John led to a business venture. Because of the high capital cost of buying and stocking land, we cast about for other ways to make our fortunes. We asked our chartered accountants, 'Which small businesses make money?' Both said, 'Bakers and butchers.' We decided we would, as progressive young men, become the first self-service butchers in Dundee, and perhaps in Scotland. Union Street was a good shopping centre and an Italian restaurant was for sale with a cellar which we could use as the workshop. By this time the dreams of no capital requirements had disappeared. We borrowed all the money – £17,000. John put down some insurance shares as security for his half and I simply gave my personal guarantee. We went about the country looking at pre-wrapped food and hired a butcher called Matchet with his brother as assistant.

From day one at Janmac the till rang merrily. Older people were able to inspect the one chop they wanted without the embarrassment of saying they wanted a small one. People liked the quick self-service. My partner, John, keen on finding out what motivated the buyers, would go round asking why they had picked certain pieces – sometimes frightening little old ladies with his ingratiating smile, which appeared to them as a terrifying leer. We copied my wife's recipe for tripe and onions, which turned out to be popular, and we quickly established a very good turnover.

However, at the end of the year we had lost money. Matchet was a good butcher, but I doubt he understood the organisation of this new type of shop. We also had trouble with stealing. We successfully replaced him with a young man from Edinburgh called McIntyre who had been involved in running a baker's chain. We came into profit and opened a branch shop. John Jenkins whose insurance shares had happily trebled, then decided to buy a farm in Cambridgeshire, and wanted out. With typical generous practicality, he required nothing for his share, except release from the obligation for the overdraft. I continued to run the business.

During the Coronation year, to raise money for various things, an extraordinary rash of 'Matters of Opinion' in village halls around the county broke out. I chaired an enormous number of these. I enjoyed it greatly and it was very easy. To ensure you were thought a good Chairman all you had to do was make a few personal cracks at the experts on the panel. About the end of this marathon, in Cortachy School, I got a wooden armed chair which was too narrow for me. Knowing that the humour would appeal, when I got up I took the chair with me, put it down and said to the audience, 'I am sorry, but I have been Chairman so often, it is not just my head which is swollen.' A crack at low level, but suitable for the occasion.

In 1956 we had Suez, when Eden's Conservative government mounted its ill-fated attack on Nasser's Egypt. My view was that it was wrong to go in and foolish to come out. It drove me to think 'that something should be done'. Colonel Scott, the Chairman of the Liberals in Angus, suggested that this time I stand myself as the Liberal Candidate. My friends rallied round and we twice ran fund-raising farm fairs at Benshie. We had John Bannerman and Jo Grimond opening them and we made a great deal of money – round about £1,400 on both occasions. We put up a marquee and on the Friday night we had a dance. Then on Saturday we had a fair with sideshows, raffles and hot dog stands. An entrepreneur who had a monkey charged people for photographs of themselves with it. The monkey, however, bit Lady Morton, a distinguished member of the National Executive. In the evening we had another dance in the marquee. By Sunday morning the willing helpers were absolutely exhausted. But people also had a lot of fun.

We came a very good second in 1959, knocking the Labour Party to the bottom of the Poll, but the Tory Jim Duncan went back with a handsome majority. Jo Grimond was our only Scots MP and we were down to 5 or 6 in the House of Commons. George Kemp, a young schoolmaster who was Secretary and gave up a great deal of his time in Edinburgh to keep the Scottish organisation going, asked if I would let my name go forward as a vice chairman of the Scottish Party. I agreed to this. We needed money and we needed some sense of direction.

In 1962, a Liberal from Stonehaven called Dan Davey came to me with a plan to raise money by a postal Bingo Pool. He was willing to give up his job as a travelling salesman to run it. I consulted my friend Ken Barton who was the Liberal candidate. He thought it might work and we put up the money required. The whole thing depended upon advertising widely and this we did at some expense. The procedure was something like this: the players filled in their Bingo coupon with numbers placed on the printed numbers giving the sequence. On Sunday the game was played in public with witnesses and the winner was the one who had the nearest correct card.

The great day came when Dan Davey reported that we were now clearing £1,000 per week. I then informed Jo Grimond, leader of the Liberal Party, that I had solved the problem of finance, not only for the Scottish Liberal Party, but indeed the English as well. In 1963 £50,000 per annum was a great deal of money, and we were still growing. Jo was so excited at the thought of an end to the endless money troubles of the Party that he smoked a cigarette to calm his nerves.

The very next day disaster struck. The newspapers refused our advertisements, on the grounds that the scheme was illegal. Panic set in. Liberal candidates running an illegal gambling racket, one of them the Vice Chairman of the Party – imagine my Wee Free supporters in Sutherland! It was obvious to us that the established football pools saw us as a rival, and either exerted pressure or spread doubt about the scheme's legality. We withdrew and left it to Dan Davey to run the venture as a privately run Bingo Postal Club club which without doubt was legal.

We did this on the understanding that Dan Davey would contribute handsomely to the Liberal Party if the scaled down venture was a success. He ran a modestly prosperous club for a number of years – and gave money to a useless cancer cure – but all we succeeded in extracting for the Liberals was £2,000, and it was difficult to get that. I don't blame him, for it was his idea and we had cut and run. The Club folded eventually and Dan went back to work as a salesman. Jo Grimond wondered if the whole thing had been a figment of George Mackie's imagination, and the Liberal Party continued to struggle for money.

Later, in 1966, I was to approach the Steel Association which was under threat of re-nationalisation, at the same time as Jeremy Thorpe was trying to get money for the English Party. They didn't give him any money. But they believed we would do well in Scotland and eventually handed me a cheque for £25,000 – at today's money this must be about half a million pounds!

Almost immediately, the General Election was announced and we were unable to use the cash. Far from taking seats, I was actually to lose my own seat. I went and offered the money back; the representative of the Steel Association recoiled in horror. I put the money into a trust and it helped Liberal projects for a considerable time. There were no strings attached, we promised nothing and no favours were asked. To my knowledge, the Scottish Liberal Party has not since received a donation anything like this size.

In the late 1970s I was to think up the idea of buying a Highland cottage and raffling it, in order to raise more money. David Miller, chief executive at the time, thought Highland cottages were out of date and suggested, half seriously, that a villa in Spain would catch the imagination. I investigated villas – associated in my mind with 'Castles in Spain' – and found a beauty with a swimming pool, beside a golf course near Valencia. I checked with the SDLP (Social Democratic Liberal Party) that they would take part and I got a promise from the Treasurer of the English Liberal Party that he would promote it in their 400 active constituencies.

The SDLP sold £16,000 worth of £10 tickets. In Scotland we sold £25,000 worth. But the English Party let us down totally, with £4,000. They failed completely to promote it, in spite of being offered the lion's share of the profit. The result was that we covered the cost of the villa, but not the considerable expense. This was borne by the four members of the committee. We split it into five; I paid 40 per cent of the loss and the others paid 20 per cent each. If we had bought a Highland cottage, which we could have done at that time for a couple of thousand quid, we would have made a handsome profit. I suppose eventually one learns in these matters.

CHAPTER 13

MP for Caithness and Sutherland

I N 1961 the then leader of the Liberal Party, Jo Grimond, said to me, 'George, you should go and fight Caithness. The Tories are quarrelling amongst themselves and there is a good chance of two Tory candidates. But I do not think the present man the Liberals are thinking of adopting can win the seat.' If we did not get seats at the next election, he said, the whole party would be finished. Jo added that he was also doubtful if I myself could win against a well dug-in MP on my previous battleground of South Angus.

I reluctantly agreed to go. Although Lindsay was against it, she agreed to back me. But when I informed the grateful Committee of Caithness and Sutherland Constituency that I was willing, much to my chagrin this was not greeted with enthusiasm, least of all by the Secretary, Ian Shaw. He was a species of local dictator who had already selected a local laird called Mark Murray-Thriepland whom he thought he could control.

It is generally true that if Headquarters try to impose a candidate on a constituency, they will automatically rebel. The people of Caithness must also have been attracted by the fact that Mark lived in the constituency. Lindsay and I went up to the selection committee meeting in Helmsdale, on the border between the two counties. There, the Caithness constituents, organised by the said Ian Shaw and much the larger body, had been delegated to vote for Murray-Thriepland. But after the speeches, Sutherland, I understand, voted solidly for me and so did a number of the Caithness delegates who disregarded their instructions. I won by one vote.

Caithness and Sutherland was one of the biggest constituencies in Scotland. It stretched from John O'Groats to Lochinver and from Cape Wrath to Dornoch. Its two components were diametrically opposed. Caithness is a Norse Lowland county in the Highlands and Sutherland a pure Celtic Highland area. The great event in these parts is the main sheep sale at Lairg every autumn. Enormous numbers are sold from all over Sutherland and indeed Ross and Cromarty and it was the biggest in Britain at one time. It was the event of the year in the lives of the shepherds and indeed of the sheep farmers. A great deal of whisky was consumed, either to celebrate a successful sale or to drown the sorrow of an unsuccessful one.

There is a lovely story about a well known farmer, John Robertson of Nigg, who, while selling his sheep and whether due to drink or other causes, fell on his knees amongst the batch in the ring. The auctioneer stopped the sale and said, 'Gentlemen, I would like to point out I am only selling the sheep,' which crack was received with great good humour by the gentleman himself.

The constituency had a history of close results. The Liberal Sir Archibald Sinclair was narrowly beaten in 1945 by a Conservative carpetbagger. In 1950 the Conservative, David Robertson, narrowly won again. But he was a very aggressive constituency MP, who quarrelled with the party and fought the 1959 Election as an Independent Conservative. When he said he would retire, the Tories selected Patrick Maitland as their official candidate. But the maverick Robertson backed John Young as an Independent Conservative to succeed him.

This was what presented us with a splendid opportunity. The local Liberals, scenting a chance, were all extremely willing to work. However, Ian Shaw seemed annoyed that control of affairs had been taken out of his hands. Eventually I had to present the constituency with an ultimatum that either he went or I did. They backed me and Shaw resigned, after which things went forward very smoothly.

I disposed of the Braeroy estate, and I also sold the Janmac butcher's business and gave my wife the secondary shop, which she rented out, giving her a small extra income. I myself was left with about £12,000 of capital gain, all of which I was now to spend on getting into Parliament.

It was a period of immense hard work. Not only was I running a large part of the organisation of the Scottish Party, but also fighting a constituency well over 200 miles from my home in Angus. However, I enjoyed it. Both Lindsay and I did an enormous amount, and spent a very large amount of money, travelling up and down and round the constituency for over three years. We ran all sorts of moneymaking social events and had an absolutely excellent advertising campaign where a photo of Liberals from different districts would appear in the local paper, saying why they were voting Liberal at the next election. Hardly a week passed but I was in Caithness or Sutherland and very often we took the family up as well. Lindsay did a power of work and was able to operate on her own. She was, of course, very much better than me in visits to hospitals and sales of work. She acquired a pretty good knowledge of Liberal policy, although I think that probably her good looks and charm did more for the acquisition of support.

One press correspondent wrote a very amusing article about the Liberal candidate who used his elegant wife and charming daughters to win the seat. Of course, they were a great help, but it was going a little too far to say that policy and the enormous amount of work put in counted for nothing against their charm.

I was fortunate in securing a really good agent. Bill Murchie had just returned to the UK from tea planting in India. He could break down and identify the types of tea after one sip. But he also played a big part in our eventual victory. Robin Sinclair (later Lord Thurso) and his wife Margaret were also very helpful.

Captain Ian Campbell of Balblair, Major Rutherford of Proncy, and John Robertson of Castle Craig were what you might call 'Patriarchs of Sutherland'. When I started canvassing in 1961, I realised that I had to get the support of senior members of the farming population. Ian Campbell had been a President of the Farmers Union and was a friend of my father's, a staunch Conservative. Major Rutherford was another very able farmer with a splendid record in the first war. I had been at University with his son Gideon, sharing the same digs in Aberdeen.

I called on Captain Campbell in the bungalow to which he had retired, leaving the main house to his son, Colin. He welcomed me and poured me a large Clynelish of which he kept a private supply from his shares in the Distillery. After this one, of course, I had to have a second enormous Clynelish, which I had happily. I then declined the third and departed in good order, although I certainly would not have passed any breath test. This was viewed with a good deal of favour by the old Captain. The Conservative candidate had apparently accepted a third and got over voluble.

When I went to see Major Rutherford, I was prepared. As he had heard from his old friend that I could carry my drink, I was able to accept a third and became rather cheerful, although still well under control. I doubt very much whether they actually brought themselves to vote for me, but there is no shadow of doubt that their approval of me and my wife as people carried a lot of weight in that district. Anyhow, they were men whom I admired greatly.

Two of my main supporters in Sutherland were Major Dudgeon

148 Squadron reunion in 1947.

My parents' 40th wedding anniversary 1947.

The house, Benshie.

Benshie steading.

Tractors and staff in the 60s.

With my young manager Graham Scrymgeour and grazing bullocks.

Outside the front door of Benshie.

A good crop of Golden Wonders.

My outdoor Wessex sows.

131

My parents' 60th wedding anniversary.

The family (less Jeannie) in a jeep at Braeroy.

Jeannie at Benshie.

Lindsay receiving flowers at a local school prizegiving.

*Jo Grimond, Johnnie Bannerman and myself at
a dinner held in Johnnie's honour.*

Canvassing fishermen in Wick.

(Geordie) and his wife Mary. He had the nice estate of Crakaig which had some good arable land lying right down to the coast and a hill of 3,000 or 4,000 acres lying behind. It lies about three or four miles south of Helmsdale. They had a beach – the water might perhaps be a little cold for all but the hardiest of the young, but they had a small caravan site on it. The house sat looking out to sea with the steading behind at one side. Mary was a good gardener and a great character. Whenever she organised any function, you could be certain that it would be extraordinarily well done. The house was always full of dogs, not always as well trained as they might be, but full of warmth. We used their house a great deal for functions and stayed frequently. Geordie was a good farmer and I was extremely grateful for his unfailing support and friendship. He died far too young, but Mary is still there doing good work and indeed has established a museum centre which my son-in-law, John Hope, designed. I hope she continues for many years to come.

George Mackay was a leading Liberal in Wick, an ex-fisherman who owned and ran the local ice factory. He was a great character with a very nice and clever wife. He was really my main activist in Wick. He introduced me to a host of people and guided me in the prejudices of the fishermen and their particular quirks. George had a share in a boat which was skippered by a superb fisherman called Norrie Brebner who was totally up-to-date in his knowledge of how to use radar to find the shoals and this, along with his inborn skill, made him and his crew extremely prosperous. The tradition and custom was very straight-forward – half the money from the catch went to the boat and reimbursed the owners of the shares in the boat who would certainly be the skipper himself and people like George, who was his uncle. The crew might or might not have shares in the boat but the other half was divided equally between the crew which included the skipper. This always appeared to me to be unfair because so much depended on the skill of the skipper. If he owned the whole of the boat himself, he was amply rewarded, but if he did not, it seemed to me quite wrong that he only received the same as the youngest member of the crew. Nevertheless, it worked well, except that the improvident members of the crew spent all their money when times were good, and when times were bad and the weather was bad, they drew the dole. George knew them all and their strengths and weaknesses. He was a power of strength in Wick and he did me a lot of good.

One of the first people George Mackay introduced me to was Miss Thain, who was a retired teacher, living with her two unmarried sisters in their good house built by her father who had been a successful fishing skipper. They were rather terrifying until you got to know them, when you found that Miss Thain in particular had an amazing sense of humour. They were genuine old Liberals, who had actual Liberal sentiments and were extremely kind to me and indeed to my daughters when they were up canvassing for me. Nice people!

I have already mentioned the Campbell from the crofting township who became Archbishop of Glasgow, leaving behind his older brother who ran the croft and played his part in the club farm, although himself a man of brains and ability. The stories of crofters' sons going to university, becoming able administrators throughout the world, and professors or politicians, are well known, but the eldest son was often of even greater ability and made his mark at home. One such was Angus Mackay who lived in Rogart in Sutherland, and was headman or secretary of the local club farm.

One of the great weaknesses of the club farms was that at the end of the year all the surplus was shared out amongst the individual members. Angus Mackay in Rogart saw this very clearly and persuaded his members to leave a portion of their share in order to improve grazing, put up fencing and do other things that would eventually bear fruit for the club members. The Inland Revenue, that dreadful body of bloodsuckers, latched on to this and said this was a company and therefore must pay tax on the money that had been laid aside for the various improvements. Angus went to the MP, Sir David Robertson, who took up the case with his usual aggressive energy and eventually won by forcing the Revenue to admit that this money was actually the property and earnings of the individual crofters who, because of their low earnings, paid no tax. Angus Mackay was a lifelong Liberal, but after this he was a strong supporter of Sir David Robertson. Happily, he switched back to Liberal again when I came up.

He was an assessor with the Crofters Commission and was called upon to settle a dispute involving an English proprietor of an estate up beside Melvich, which is Mackay country. The proprietor was fighting with his tenants, all of whom were Mackays. There was a good deal of acrimony, and I have no doubt that the tenants were being quite as unreasonable as the landlord. Anyhow, they were walking on the hill during the inspection and they came upon an old graveyard so they went in to inspect the stones and Angus remarked to the proprietor, 'Ah, a lot of Mackays here.' Whereupon the reply was, 'Not nearly enough,' which at least showed a sense of humour. Angus never told me if he settled the dispute as this was too good a story to spoil.

In Sutherland one of my main supporters and a very good personal friend was Alec MacLeod. He was a native of the county who had been in the Police and on leaving the Police Force had got the job of District Clerk in Rogart. He was a real staunch, upright man who, furthermore, was a genuine Liberal, actually believing in that intolerant county that Roman Catholics should be allowed to worship God as they pleased. He did an enormous amount of work and took me round the West where he knew a large number of people. He was always on my side, the reason being that if he was against any project, I was pretty sure it was wrong and we discussed the thing very thoroughly. Like most people in the North, he liked a dram, but could always carry it. He had an excellent mind and it was a great sorrow to me when he took a stroke from which he never really recovered.

In Sutherland particularly, Liberalism had a very strong base in anti-landlordism stemming, and rightly, from the Clearances which were particularly brutal on the Sutherland Estates. Nothing the Sutherlands subsequently tried to do by way of starting woollen mills, providing work of all sorts, has ever eradicated this feeling which found its cohesion in the Liberal Party and later in the Labour Party, so that many of my supporters had totally illiberal ideas about hanging, flogging and many other anti-Liberal sentiments. It was therefore a joy and delight to find a number of people who, though far from approving of the young Liberals of the time, were genuine and staunch Liberals. Alec MacLeod was one of these and I salute his memory.

We had a very good following among the 'atomic' population of Thurso. Two excellent ladies there – Patsy Meiklejohn and Mal Coul – once went canvassing in the deep country. They came to an old cottage and the door was answered by a lady of eighty summers, brown as a berry and smoking a clay pipe. Mal Coul launched into an exposition of Liberal policy, including our support for the EEC, but after a minute and a half realised that this was not going over big so she stopped and said, 'Anyhow, you should vote for George Mackie. He is the best man.' Thereupon the old woman's eyes gleamed and she seized Mal's arm and said, 'How do you ken? Have you tried him?'

The people of the John O'Groats area too, were mainly Labour or

Liberal, with about two brave Conservatives. Meetings there were immensely lively and most enjoyable – if you could handle them! Jock Mowat was perhaps my main supporter there, a very tough crofter and fisherman. He and his wife introduced me to eating a newly boiled crab with a spoon.

One of the great strokes of luck I had was in making friends with Bert and Elizabeth Mowat of the Portland Arms Hotel, Lybster. The hotel had been in the family for a hundred years, but he also ran the local mart, the premises of which were at the back. When I arrived I was told that he was selling sheep. Just as I got beside the ring, an old ewe jumped over the rail, practically into my arms. I caught it and swung it back into the ring, thereby earning a nod and a word of thanks from Bert and proving a splendid introduction. We then found that we had both served in the RAF during the War and our friendship was cemented.

I came back there about 1.30 a.m. one night with Jo Grimond after a meeting in Sutherland – to find a bottle of admirable hock in the fridge and a cold lobster apiece with mayonnaise awaiting us. Jo was green with envy and said, 'My God, why can't they shift over to Orkney?' We were to have many splendid parties in the Portland.

We had one or two false starts in the campaign. I kept hoping for a quick election, but the Tories hung on until the last minute after Alec Douglas-Home became Prime Minister. They needed all the time they could to build up his name. However, the sitting Conservative MP, Sir David Robertson, was so infuriated by the local party having neglected his advice as to the candidate that he threatened to resign. We would have won a by-election with great ease but frustratingly for us, he never actually did so.

I was also unfortunate enough to break my leg rather badly while skiing at Aviemore in 1963. I was loosening up, preparing to go to St Moritz, where I hoped to go down the Cresta Run. Twelve men carried me off the mountain and I was treated. But when I eventually saw George Hay, the skilful orthopaedic chief at Stracathro hospital – having been taken there through the snow in a tattie van borrowed for the occasion – he took one look at the X-ray and immediately reset the leg, driving pins through the top and bottom to get the length right. This was successful and I had no limp.

The news reached Caithness of course. My Conservative opponent Patrick Maitland from the platform declared his sympathy, saying what a nice chap George Mackie was, and what a pity that he broke his leg skiing on the Sabbath Day! The fact is that I skied safely on the Sabbath Day and only broke it on the Monday. It took some time to mend, but I was quite quickly about on crutches and back to the campaign, hoping for a sympathy vote.

Patrick Maitland put a terrific amount of work in as Tory candidate, producing all sorts of wonderful schemes such that for a great city of the north on the beautiful Loch Eribol. This indeed could well have been a staging post for shipping, but certainly it would have spoiled the beautiful wilderness. And by the time it came to the election we really were well organised, much, much better than the Conservatives and a little better than the Labour Party.

The period from 1961 until the Election in 1964 was one of concentration of effort by the whole Scottish Liberal organisation; we targeted all the Highland constituencies. There was a strong residual feeling for the Liberals there. We had Jo Grimond, our sole MP and leader, in Orkney and Shetland, of course. We had an admirable selection of candidates in the other seats, most of whom came in because they were influenced by Jo Grimond's intellectual exposition of Liberal philosophy. We published a booklet on our plans for the Highlands, advocating in some detail a Highland Development Authority on the lines of the Tennessee Valley Authority.

A number of us contributed, but we made Russell Johnston the Editor, and I think this helped his general image. There is no doubt at all that while it is true that usually in a General Election, a very good Tory or Labour candidate is not worth more than an extra 5 per cent, the personality of the Liberal candidate is absolutely vital for success. We went to a great deal of trouble to get the right people in the right places. Inverness seemed our most winnable seat. Russell Johnston, who was a schoolmaster, had been adopted. It was obvious that he had a great deal of work to do. We therefore appointed him as Research Officer. He was particularly good on transport and did some very useful research on it for the party. But this also enabled him to really be a full-time candidate. Russell was brought up in Skye and already had a very good knowledge of the whole constituency.

Donnie MacLeod, a very popular journalist, stood for the Western Isles. I was in Caithness and Sutherland, and John Mackay (who subsequently went to the Tories) in Argyll and Bute. We also had David Steel in the Borders and Alasdair Mackenzie in Ross and Cromarty. We provided and paid for an organiser and a mini van as his constituency organisation was not strong. He was a very popular local man, and although I would not have said that his Liberal instincts were particularly up to date, this was to carry him to victory.

Those were the seats that we thought we had a chance of winning. In Greenock, which was our only hope in the West, we had Campbell Barclay. Bill Riddell was the Provost there and had done sterling work. The West Aberdeenshire seat turned out to be a particular example of what a good candidate can eventually achieve. I attended a meeting of four persons in Alford in my capacity as Chairman of the Organisation Committee. The others were a young schoolmaster who was a hard worker for the party, a local merchant who was popular and influential, and Jim Davidson, an ex-naval officer who was farming in the area. At that 'representative' meeting we arranged for Jim to be candidate and his energy and obvious ability were to show an excellent result in 1964. He won the seat in 1966. The same was certainly true of David Steel in the Borders.

The history of the Borders constituency is very interesting. We had a Liberal MP there just after the war but it had been held for some years by the Conservatives. Interest was reviving in the Constituency Association and they were determined to get a good candidate. As chairman of the Organisation Committee I found them annoying, because they considered themselves the most hopeful seat in Scotland. The only candidate they wanted had to be a carbon copy of Jo Grimond or the young Gladstone. They turned down a number of very good young candidates, including Russell Johnston, but eventually brought themselves to consider David Steel, who was then doing extremely well as the candidate for Edinburgh Pentlands. It stuck out a mile to me that Pentlands was not a winnable seat in the near future and that the sooner the Borders had a candidate the better. David was dead keen to go as he had an admirable political nose and knew that he could win Roxburgh, Selkirk and Peebles.

Pentland Constituency Party were extremely unwilling to lose their good candidate and I arranged a meeting with David to persuade the constituency executives to release him. I thought that I had used all my skill in persuading them that for the good of the party they should release David, as if we did not win seats at the next Election, the whole party was finished. I noticed them nodding agreement round the table and said, 'We will leave you to consider it, and of course, it is your decision,' hoping that I had won the day. However the Constituency did not voluntarily relinquish their good candidate. David was adopted by the Borders and I arranged a vote of censure to be passed by the Executive on myself for my 'over-bearing' attitude to Pentlands Constituency which settled the matter to everyone's satisfaction.

After three and a half years hard work, it was a great relief and excitement to approach the Election which was held at the last possible date. There was general disillusionment with a long period of Tory Government. (Although I may say, looking back now, I realise that they were angels of mercy compared to the Thatcherite on-the-make Tories to come.) At the last minute the Labour Party rushed out a poor copy of our Highland Development plan on a single sheet of white paper.

We had studied the constituency over the long period of preparation, and we knew exactly where we would have meetings. If you missed a small village, although only two or three people would come, they deeply resented the fact that you had ignored their area.

We opened the campaign with an advantage, for we had lots of quotes in the national press, who thought we might well win: *Sunday Express* – 'Liberals should gain two seats. Cornwall and Caithness and Sutherland.' *Scottish Daily Express* – 'The greatest turn-up of all, and it will surprise no one, would be the return of Scotland's second Liberal MP, George Mackie.' *Glasgow Herald* – 'Prospects for a Liberal victory in the far North have never been better.' *Press and Journal* – 'I should not be too surprised if, on the taxi ride to Westminster, George Mackie is not taking up more than his fair share of room in the back seat.' *The Times* – 'The Liberal Party are infinitely stronger than they have ever been in my memory.' *The Local Bookie* – 'Favourite – Mackie 5-4' (I made sure I was the favourite.)

From the Portland Arms we proceeded each morning, sometimes in different directions because Lindsay had her visits to hospitals and schools. We did a lot of door-to-door canvassing, although our time for this was strictly limited by the long distances we had to cover for meetings. The signs were very hopeful. I remember, however, going to one door which was opened by a small man who glared at me with hatred on his face. When I said, 'I am George Mackie,' he screwed his face up in an appalling grimace, spat on the floor and slammed the door. I put him down on my card as 'doubtful'.

By Election Day, we had a list of every potential Liberal voter and any number of helpers with cars, and I think we were able to get the maximum turn-out. Certainly one of my Tory farming friends was so impressed that he told me afterwards that they had never seen such organisation. But because of the vast distances, the count was not until two days later. My apprehension during the wait was considerable. On the morning of the count, for the first time, I found that my breakfast was not as appetising as it should have been. I forced it down and Lindsay and I proceeded to the count, which had been going on for about an hour and a half. There we met our supporters in a state of high excitement. They knew that we had won. The relief was enormous.

The next news that came in was that Alasdair Mackenzie had won Ross and Cromarty. Russell Johnston at Inverness-shire told me that his fits of depression got deeper and deeper, as he was sure that he would be the man to let the side down. However, all was well, and we won four seats in the Highlands. Though we did not win the Western Isles, we did very well in the Borders and Argyll. The only new seat in England was that won by Peter Bessel, who, it turned out, would certainly not have been a credit to any party.

We had obviously saved the Liberals as without the Highland seats, it would have been a miserable rout indeed. The concerted push in targeting the Highland area had caught the imagination of the people. Combined with my personal commitment to development, it had also overcome the personal image of an East Coast 'barley baron' my opponents would have liked to foster in Caithness. As a result of our Highland success, I was able to copy a phrase from Basil Wishart, the Liberal editor of the *Shetland Times* and say, 'There is not a Tory left between Muckle Flugga and Ballachulish!'

CHAPTER 14

In the Commons

WHEN I GOT DOWN to Westminster, I thought I was a picture of a smooth Member of Parliament in my best suit and watch chain, and I made my maiden speech four or five days after getting in. Jo Grimond was walking out of the House with an old Tory who said to him, 'Good speech that fellow of yours made, Jo.' And then he added, 'But by God, you can see he comes from Caithness – a great shaggy brute!'

To say I was pleased to be elected is an understatement. I took to the life like a duck to water. I felt very much at home in the House of Commons and I liked the atmosphere, I liked the work and I liked the social life.

The Scottish contingent was a small but highly significant band: Jo Grimond, Orkney and Shetland, Leader; Mackie for Caithness; Mackenzie for Ross and Cromarty; Johnston for Inverness and, later, Steel for the Borders. In Wales we had two members, Emlyn Hooson for Montgomery and Roderic Bowen for Cardigan. Jeremy Thorpe for North Devon, the one new English member, Peter Bessell, and the Chief Whip, Eric Lubbock, completed the picture, so that we had in all ten members.

This meant the Whips Office was fairly crowded. I inherited an experienced secretary, Gillian Jacombe-Hood, which was a great help. I was made Scottish Whip and shared an office with Eric Lubbock. I was also made Economic Spokesman. I eventually rented a pleasant little flat in the less smart northern end of Great Peter Street, near Westminster. Lindsay enjoyed it when she came down. But because of the new Labour government's minute majority of only one, we were kept hard at it and I never got a trip abroad. Certainly Lindsay had none of the perks which an MP's wife can have, simply because we were so busy.

One political point of importance was that there was a need to curb the excesses of our military industrial complex. The aircraft industry was doing a great deal of development on a simple cost plus 5 per cent basis, which was more than the country could stand. With only one of a majority, forcing through unpopular decisions was extremely difficult and Roy Jenkins came to Jo Grimond to ask for his support for the unpopular measure of cancelling several projects, among them the TSR II low level bomber which was in a fairly advanced state of development. This specific project may or may not have been a mistake, but the general picture of excessive use of Government funds was accurate. Jo Grimond came to me and explained. I agreed that we ought to support the Government, thinking in terms of co-operation and possible political benefit.

We then ran into trouble. Eric Lubbock was an engineer and deeply committed to research, particularly on the TSR II. Russell Johnston said he would follow his specialist advice. Bessell and Thorpe were terrified of what the Tories would say against them in the West Country. The others were fairly neutral. I regarded it as an occasion for Jo to be tough and try to force them into line, but Jo, perhaps wisely, thought it could not be done and so informed Roy Jenkins. The Cabinet then took the courageous decision that a majority of one was enough and went ahead saying, 'Damn the Liberal Party. They are not reliable and cannot deliver.' They were proven right in their gamble when they subsequently won a by-election in Hull. This set the stage for the 1966 Election which followed shortly afterwards. On the morning of the Government victory in the Hull by-election, I was walking along the back corridor and saw the Prime Minister coming towards me. I could see Harold Wilson thinking, 'Mackie. The Liberals don't count now. A short nod will do for him.' So it appeared, but by the time he made the short nod, I was grinning widely. I knew just what was coming. I turned round to look at him and there was a flush on the back of his neck as he realised that I knew what he was thinking.

The main constituency issue was the prototype nuclear fast reactor. The intention had been to site it at Windscale in Cumbria, rather than in Dounreay in my constituency. I made lots of statements and harried the Secretary of State, Willie Ross, unmercifully, so much so that a deputation of Scots Labour MPs went to the Prime Minister and demanded that Dounreay receive the PFR, as the Labour Party was the strong opposition to me in Caithness and had a great deal of support in Dounreay. By a Cabinet decision, this was done. When the Minister, Frank Cousins, announced this in the House of Commons he specifically said that social consideration and questions of employment came into the matter. There were cries from the Scottish Labour MPs, 'Where's George?' I, of course, got up and congratulated the Government on their good sense. I may say that the credit in the end went to the Labour Party and without doubt played a part in my subsequent defeat.

I did, like everyone else, a great deal of constituency work. One lady came to me in great distress because owing to road widening she was to lose a part of her much-loved garden. I went to see the road surveyor who said, 'You know, I could easily shift it without any more expense to widen the road on the other side.' And so he did. I was happy to inform the lady that I had saved her beloved garden. But a couple of months later, I had a furious letter from her. She said that I did not inform her that she would have received compensation, which the lady on the other side had got! One should not expect credit.

One of the great things in an area such as Caithness and Sutherland was to keep the harbours in good condition, and, with an enormous coastline, it was extremely expensive. The Scottish Department was really very good about it and I was constantly writing on behalf of the fishermen in remote spots for improvement to a harbour to enable perhaps only a few lobster boats to use it. I was in constant correspondence with Lord Hughes, who was the Minister of State in charge of Highland Affairs. I found him very sympathetic. When he suggested a tour during the recess, I jumped at the chance and we had a wonderful two days meeting the fishermen and seeing the harbours. Happily we got good weather. Bill Hughes was very interested, and it was a great help in future dealings to know that when a case was brought before him, he actually had seen the spot and remembered it.

Bill Hughes was an absolutely first class Minister, a practical Scot with wide experience of public work. A great deal of money was spent on the harbours there and certainly it was for the good of the trade as the lorries conveyed an enormous amount of fish along the narrow roads to the markets in the south. But while we had a number of very good fishermen working out of Wick, Thurso and Helmsdale and Lybster, the bulk of the fishing on the West coast was actually done by East coast fishermen from Banffshire and Aberdeenshire. They took their boats over to Kinlochbervie or Lochinver, fished out of there all week and went home by car at the weekend. They were very enterprising, very hard-working, and it was a pity that more of the native West Highland men could not be persuaded or helped to fish in the same way. The fact was that most enterprise shown in that area seemed to come from outside.

West Sutherland from Lochinver north to Cape Wrath and round to Eriboll and Tongue is the most beautiful country but had a tremendous sadness about it. The tradition was of the vigorous and the clever leaving either for Glasgow and London or the colonies. Eventually, of course, many crofts were abandoned. You can see the results at deserted spots like Elphin near Inchnadamph – one of the saddest such places I have ever known. Emigration was not always as harmful as it appeared. Such was the love of the land and the croft that the eldest son would always be the one to stay behind to run the family home. He was often more vigorous and indeed much cleverer than the younger son who did well in far away places. But there were curious colonies round the coast where many crofters belonged to the Free Presbyterian Church, with its extraordinarily narrow views and a sort of fanatical piety only alleviated by bursts of drinking.

The hand of the landlord also lay quite heavily on the spirit of the people. The history of the Clearances had been handed down through the generations and the feeling was still very strong. Sporting land-lords did put a great deal of money into the Highlands for their pleasure, and depopulation would have been greater without them. They did not, however, do anything for the genuine rehabilitation of the area.

In Lochinver a new pottery started and was doing well and East coast fishermen were providing some prosperity along with the ordinary tourist all summer. The salmon fishing contribution was significant. The coming of the Highland Board whereby, with the co-operation of British Telecom, they have set up a complete system of telecom-munications throughout the Highlands, thereby later enabling the most modern computer systems to be set up all over the area, may well be bearing fruit too.

But my own experience is that it is difficult to make people of the right age go to the Highlands and leave the social life of the south, whether for their own sakes or for the sakes of their children. And when local children from the age of 11 had to go to the East coast and be boarded out for their secondary schooling, it had a very adverse affect on employment. The East coast schools at Golspie and Dornoch did a very good job and the children boarding were well looked after and enjoyed themselves, but many shepherds or keepers wanted to move when their children got to that age so that they could stay at home. I was very conscious of this and did a good deal of work studying educational systems in Norway, Australia and other places with remote populations. I went to Judith Hart, the Minister in charge of education in Scotland, with a good deal of evidence that a plan could be produced to keep children in the West, at least until they were 15, by introducing incentives for good teachers to go there and have a system of travelling specialists. They would visit the small schools to supplement the resident teachers. There was a lot of evidence that when the children from country schools went to senior secondary, they out-performed the children from the more populous areas, although it took them a little time to settle down. Judith Hart listened to me until my allotted half hour was up and then turned with ill-concealed relief back to her conventional papers.

In common with all Members of Parliament, some tragic and fascinating human stories came my way. Many of these were connected with crofting, the succession to crofts and compensation with regard to improvements. Life in the beautiful crofting areas was not always idyllic. People sometimes came from elsewhere in Scotland to inherit the tenancy for a croft and left later, disillusioned with the life.

One such case ended very nastily. A lady had come up to a croft in the Doll – an area of level plain lying into the hills behind Brora. She was on her own with a son and three daughters. She farmed it for a number of years before finding it too much, and she then let the land to a neighbouring crofter, who was a good neighbour and helped her. She, however, kept a few sheep for herself on the croft. During the lambing season she lost a ewe which had triplets. One lamb then died and she was left with two bottle-fed lambs in a pen over the back garden wall. On this day in May she had to go to Inverness to visit another daughter in hospital. The good neighbour came over to bottle-feed the lambs. He found that one of the two remaining lambs had died. Thereupon he noticed that another neighbour had triplets on a ewe. He caught one of the triplets and substituted it for the lady's dead lamb. He did this out of kindness and no doubt thinking that the crofter who actually owned the lamb and who was living at some distance away would never notice. He also dabbed both lambs with her red mark.

The act of kindness brought great trouble. The other crofter noticed his ewe had only two lambs and did not find a dead one, so he brought the Sergeant of Police out. They ran the lamb with the ewe now left with twins and the ewe took to it. This was considered proof, as indeed it was. The lady was then charged, along with her nice neighbour, with theft of the lamb. The worry caused her to have a cerebral haemorrhage and, owing to her treatments in Inverness and Aberdeen Infirmaries, the case was postponed until October. Although the good neighbour admitted the theft of the lamb, her solicitor was very displeased with the lady because her form for legal aid had been handed in late and he appeared to make a thorough mess of the case. They were not called and neither was found guilty of theft, but she was found guilty of reset and fined £10. The lady's son had to come home from sea when she was in hospital and her schoolgirl daughters were much distressed as none can be more cruel than children. She went to another solicitor, who advised her to write to me.

I am aware of the feeling about sheep stealing and the necessity for taking strong measures to stop it, but to me there is little doubt that the lady in question had no idea that a lamb had been stolen. Her neighbour's good intentions did a lot of harm, however, and he should certainly have been fined. I found that I could do nothing about having the case reopened, but that it might be possible to get a pardon. Having received an affidavit from the nice neighbour, I wrote to the Secretary of State. But the Procurator Fiscal was hostile to the whole idea and this led to the Secretary of State's decision. His reply was that he could not consider recommendation to Her Majesty for a pardon for the victim of this appalling miscarriage of justice. She left the area and got a job in the south of Scotland near Newton Stewart, where I hope she was better treated than she was in the Highlands.

Alcoholism is another great problem in the Highlands. The causes are complex, but it has certainly to do with the northern latitude and an attitude towards whisky amongst the young. There were no bars at dances and the taking of a half bottle to drink outside the hall I think was a vicious habit and far removed from social drinking. Alcoholism extended, however, to all classes of society.

When doctors took to drink, it frequently led to trouble. I had a very sad case of a young woman who appeared to be in good health. But her doctor, it seemed, sent her to hospital long before her baby was due. Everyone knew that the doctor in question was an alcoholic. After attempts at inducing the baby, the doctor in the hospital recognised that it was not in fact due. She went home with instructions to return to hospital in eight or nine days time, or when she went into labour. Four days later she went into labour at home, allegedly at her own wish. The child died after a complicated labour. A haemorrhage necessitated the mother being taken to hospital, where she died a few minutes after admission. The words used by the Secretary of State when I brought the case to the attention were, 'My Chief Medical Officer has...been given access to detailed confidential information about the conduct of the case and is entirely satisfied that any allegation of neglect or bad practice could not be sustained. I see no basis for further enquiry.' The husband and the parents were prevented from making a complaint at the time because they themselves were responsible for allowing the young woman to come home. But it is also true that there was a curious reluctance among others to come forward. I wrote to my friend and supporter, the Convener of the County, Mr John Mackay of Bighouse. His reply was very interesting:

> I am perfectly sure it would be impossible to get people in this area to come forward to give evidence against this doctor in front of a tribunal for although they all know and have seen him on duty while under the influence of drink and will talk about his condition, there is that something about the doctor which makes it most difficult for anyone to give evidence which would finish him as a Practitioner. My own personal opinion is that his usefulness as a doctor in the parish has long since passed and on many occasions his patients have a lean time...I do not think the action of the Department can inspire the man in the street with any confidence that his legitimate grievance received any consideration whatsoever. The Sutherland Executive Council and possibly the Department are well aware that this doctor is a confirmed alcoholic and should not be left in sole charge of a rural practice.

The Labour Government victory in the 1966 by-election in Hull and their rising popularity in the country made it obvious that Wilson was not going to tolerate a minute majority for much longer, and sure enough an announcement of the Election came soon afterwards. Labour were doing well in my constituency. The most unhappy set of circumstances also occurred. First of all, I had persuaded Robin Sinclair in my capacity as chairman of the Organisation Committee of the Scottish party to go as a candidate to East Aberdeenshire, as we were determined to fight as many seats as possible. Robin's wife Margaret, who was very popular, accompanied her husband on his campaign there. Worse than that, he then decided to resign as Chairman of Thurso and, by a piece of appalling neglect, allowed Ian Shaw, the ex-Secretary, who hated me with a pure and passionate hatred because I had forced him to resign, to succeed him as Chairman of the Thurso Branch.

I needed an organiser. In the selection process, I had thrown in one very unfortunate character – on whose face was written his liking for strong drink – as make-weight in order to balance the rather good young ex-Tory organiser I wanted to engage. The meeting to, as I thought, select my candidate for organiser took place in the Portland Arms Hotel in Lybster, which was over the hill from Sutherland county. There was a snowstorm on the night and the Sutherland contingent couldn't get over the Ord.

The new Chairman of Thurso, Ian Shaw, persuaded the Caithness contingent that it was wrong to take a young man with a family as this was an insecure job. He urged they should take the older man as the appointee. This was an extremely cunning move as he turned out to be totally incompetent. Having foolishly left it to the committee, I was unable to reverse the decision. I should have convened a full meeting, but didn't, so we went into the Election with a hostile Chairman in Thurso and an incompetent agent.

The Labour Party then selected a new candidate. The previous candidate in '64 had been totally unsuitable. He was a Glasgow Trade Unionist with no knowledge whatsoever of the area. His wife, in fact, would have been a far better candidate. I reckon he was worth at least 1,000 votes from the Labour supporters to me. This time the Labour Party selected Robert MacLennan. He was absolutely hopeless on the platform, but he appealed to the Labour Party. He was then a good looking young man whose father was a knight and a surgeon in Glasgow, and who had connections with the constituency through Sutherland. This, combined with the national swing to Labour, made the situation fairly marginal. Wilson actually told Jeremy Thorpe that they were going to win Caithness. (Thorpe somehow neglected to pass this information on to me.)

The Tories put out the story that my voting record was 'only' 74 per cent – I had missed out on 26 per cent of the votes in the House of Commons, thus neglecting my duty. I immediately looked up the figures and found that my voting record was better than any Conservative MP. It silenced that particular story. However, it is very difficult to control one's own supporters. The schoolmaster in Embo, Sutherland, beside Dornoch, was a very good Liberal and totally indignant about it. Instead of letting things be after I had effectively silenced the story, when I had a meeting there he got up and introduced me in glowing terms as a good MP and finished by saying, 'And now George Mackie will tell you what a lie the Tories put out when they said he had only voted in 74 per cent of the votes.' I therefore had to explain the whole thing to a puzzled audience.

I thought there was a good story in visiting Cape Wrath to canvass the lighthouse men there. I accordingly arranged with the press to meet me and we took the boat over the ferry and proceeded in a little bus over bad roads and in a howling gale. When we got there, I, at 6' 4" and 17 stone, could lean into the wind at an angle of nearly 45 degrees, but Lindsay was nearly blown away. However, we met the lighthouse men and some good pictures were taken. It served its purpose in that the *Daily Express* next day included a picture and the headline was 'By George's Wrath!' But it turned out that not a single one of them had a vote in Caithness and Sutherland.

We fought a good campaign. Again, Lindsay and the family were an enormous help and did a great deal of work. One or two of my supporters were also conscious of the rise in the Labour vote, but in the main throughout the country parts of the constituency and Sutherland they were confident of winning again – perhaps over-confident. When we went into the count, we knew that there had been a big swing to Labour in the country and we also knew that another snowstorm on the north coast had kept many of my own country supporters at home. The traditional knife-edge situation was apparent. In the end we lost by 64 votes after a re-count.

R.A.R. MacLennan – Labour	8,308	39.2%
G.Y. Mackie – Liberal	8,244	38.9%
J.M. Watt – Conservative	4,662	22.0%
Labour Majority	64	0.3%

Again, I made a mistake, in that I asked for a check of the bundles but did not ask for a complete revision. Yet I doubt if it would have made any difference.

It is ironic but in 1966 I put up my percentage of the vote and lost the seat. The only other colleague to raise his percentage, and that by less than me, was Alasdair Mackenzie. This is entirely irrelevant and put in to salve my hurt pride, for the fact is there are no second prizes in politics.

CHAPTER 15

The Scottish Liberals

J o Grimond had been desperately disappointed with the Liberal Party's election results in 1964. His campaign efforts in the Highlands had been quite exemplary. He did a tour whenever he was asked, often speaking to very few people in remote places. He had put a terrific effort into the leadership and had got many very good young people in the universities interested. But the trouble with leading the Liberal Party in the last two-thirds of this century has been that it is all uphill – like climbing a mountain, you surmount a tough ridge and there you see another in front of you.

Towards the end of 1964 Jo took me aside and said he was thinking of giving up the leadership. I urged him to stay on. Jeremy Thorpe was also in Jo's confidence. Above all else he wanted to be leader. Jeremy had very strong Liberal convictions, but was very much in the traditional vein of British politics which he had absorbed in the rarefied atmosphere of Eton and the Oxford Union. Even during his years at the Bar, his whole life was devoted to politics. He therefore saw part of the glittering prize within his grasp and when someone told him that I might be standing for the leadership, he hauled me into his car in New Palace Yard in a state of great excitement. He said, 'If you do, I will beat you into the ground, but if you support me, I will make you Deputy Leader.' I burst out laughing and left the car still helpless with laughter. I was totally against Jeremy as leader because, although he was a magnificent campaigner, he was lightweight and too fond of the tinsel.

Jo did not in the end retire until after the 1966 Election, so when we had an election amongst the MPs for the leader, I was out of Parliament. The three candidates were Eric Lubbock, Emlyn Hooson and Jeremy Thorpe. Eric Lubbock I liked and admired, but did not think him suitable. I thought the best available was Emlyn – regarded as a brilliant Queen's Counsel with a glittering career in front of him at the Bar which, if elected, he was quite willing to give up. Laura Grimond telephoned me, furious that I was backing Hooson. There was a strong touch of the old battle between Lloyd George and Asquith and between their daughters Megan and Violet. One of the newly elected MPs was Jim Davidson, whose vote was crucial, and I came down to London to try to influence him. Unfortunately, Jo Grimond got hold of him first and persuaded him that the English party would never accept Hooson and that Thorpe was the man. The vote split six for Jeremy, three for Hooson and three for Lubbock and on the second round Jeremy was elected. His essential weakness of character then led ultimately to the disaster in which he was tried at the Old Bailey for conspiracy to murder a young man who claimed to have been his lover. Despite his acquittal, it led to Thorpe's political eclipse.

The subsequent battle for the leadership then was between David Steel and John Pardoe. Pardoe, a West Country MP, made the mistake of alleging that, because he was a bit of a bastard, that made him suitable for taking the party through the difficult period that lay ahead. We all had lots of fun with this and I wrote a ditty about it.

> Pardoe's crude – but he will fight,
> Scattering shot to left and right.
> The fight will be uncommon rough
> But Libs will by the end be tough.
> Libs will grasp the Grail elusive,
> By mastery of the arts abusive.
> Must we – to gather votes in season
> Abandon now the use of reason?
> Perhaps young Steel can break the deadlock
> Although, alas, he's born in wedlock!

David won by a handsome margin and led the party with great effect for ten years.

The Scottish Liberal party was much in need of a good organising secretary and we advertised. Among the applications to succeed him was one from an ex-RAF Squadron Leader, Arthur Purdom. He interviewed in a curiously taut manner and did not impress a couple of the committee. But I myself was thoroughly prejudiced in his favour, thinking that I saw behind his rather formal style. I managed to push the appointment through. He and I got on extremely well as we were both fond of what he called 'an occasional injection' – and of course the joint background of the RAF was a help. He introduced new systems into the office, but kept them simple, and proceeded to acquire a wide knowledge of the people in all parts of Scotland where we worked.

I enjoyed working with Arthur Purdom and, as always happens with hard work, we also had a great deal of fun. On one occasion we were down in London with Lord Byers. We had twenty minutes of quick decisions in the Frank Byers style, then, when we finished, he closed his file and left the room. When he got outside the door, he must have remembered that his nice wife, Joan, had told him to be polite to people, because the door opened suddenly and he pushed his head round and barked, 'Goodbye.' Arthur and I were both flattered and amused.

The real highlight of Arthur's career in the Scottish Liberal Party was David Steel's by-election in the Borders. We really put everything we had into it and had volunteers from all over Scotland. The Tories concentrated their efforts in Galashiels. Arthur kept the office in Galashiels down to a minimum and his helpers were put round the area from Peebles to Hawick, working on the ground, with the result that our opponents never really knew the intensity of the Liberal effort. I was absolutely certain that we were going to win and put a £1,500 bet on with Ladbrokes. Very happily, it came off. David was the Member there for over thirty years before coming to the House of Lords, and then became 'Speaker' in the Scots Parliament.

Arthur Purdom himself subsequently became extremely unhappy over the issue of collaboration with the Scot Nats. Although we both wanted a Scottish Parliament, he knew the Scot Nats in the main were wholly illiberal. He resigned, and he died far too young some years later.

Johnny Bannerman, another figure in the Scottish Liberals, was a great man. He played rugby for Scotland 32 times, 16 times as captain. He was a Glasgow Gael with his roots in the Highlands and factor to the old Duke of Montrose – I am not sure whether Johnny infected the Duke with his strong Scottish feeling or the Duke infected Johnny, but I suspect it was the former. In addition to being a splendid leader, he won a gold medal at the Mod – some said it was not the quality of his voice, but the feeling he poured into the song. He was a wonderful speaker, feeling his way until he found the right note when the words poured forth in a lucid and tuneful torrent. Above all, he was a warm man and full of courage. I went to see him when he was dying and instead of me cheering him up, he cheered me.

He had his faults. He was not a particularly good organiser and at times looked upon me with great suspicion in that he thought that I was a 'barley baron' from the East coast and could not possibly understand the feelings of the Highland crofter. We often disagreed, but never quarrelled. He realised that I had a certain organising ability, and, of course, I held him in the highest regard. His political instincts in the West of Scotland were very sound and his devotion to the party transcended his personal interest.

He had for many years carried the banner in Inverness-shire and would have won it at the next Election. However, a by-election came up in Paisley. We could not get a suitable candidate and were about to reluctantly stand down. Johnny said that he would stand himself. This, of course, made a tremendous difference to the whole affair. We worked hard, but we could have worked harder and got more people in if we had known, what Johnny smelt, that he was near victory; so near that at the count the Labour candidate was so overcome that he had to go out to recover himself. Johnny had to promise to stand again at the next election which, of course, being a General Election, he had little hope of winning. We then had to find another candidate for Inverness and put in Russell Johnston. He won the seat while Paisley was held by the Labour Party.

Johnny, by way of consolation, got the first peerage which Jeremy Thorpe was offered. But the real crown of his public life was the respect and devotion in which he was held by the people of Scotland. I remember having a ceilidh in my constituency in the little coastal town of Golspie. Suddenly the word got round that John Bannerman was coming. You could feel a wave of excitement sweep through the audience and there was no let down when Johnny arrived. He immediately enthused the whole affair by the force of his personality.

Amongst the rugby-playing fraternity, there are many stories about him. In the glorious amateur days between the Wars the Scottish team were proceeding by train to play an International. Johnny got all the forwards together in the carriage, proceeded to lecture them on tactics and finished by saying, 'And remember, we must tackle these damned Irish forwards hard.' Someone said, 'Johnnie, we are playing Wales.' Without batting an eyelid, Johnnie said, 'It comes to the same thing.' They went on to win.

He was a particularly good chairman in that if someone put a point of order, he would sweep it aside with such good humour that the nit-picker had no chance at all. Mark you, if a debate got up on a subject on which he felt keenly, there was no question of the impartiality of the chair; he went full out for the side he believed in.

His funeral was the most tremendous tribute. The Gaelic Church was packed to the door, there was wonderful singing by the Glasgow Gaelic Choir and tears were seen to run down the cheeks of that tough organiser from the deep south, Frank Byers. After the service, the police manned all the crossings on the route to the churchyard at Drymen, where another thousand people had gathered for his burial.

His daughter, Rae Michie, won the Argyll and Bute constituency in the 1988 Election and held it again in 1992 and 1997 to our great delight, but I knew the biggest joy she had in winning the seat was the fact that her father would have been delighted.

CHAPTER 16

Caithness Glass

I BECOME Chairman of Caithness Glass while I was an MP after, in 1965, being approached by Robin Sinclair, afterwards Lord Thurso. He had founded Caithness Glass by raising £50,000 (which in the late 50s and early 60s was a great deal of money) from shareholders all over Scotland. He then got the Government to build him a factory which the new Company rented. He got hold of an Irish designer, mainly trained in Scandinavia, and some Italian glass blowers, hired four apprentices and started making glass in a variety of colours, most of which was attractive in a rather Scandinavian way.

The £50,000 was quickly swallowed up by what was perhaps a rather too ambitious start and Robin then got Lord Runciman to come in with extra money and the first shareholders' money took second place to the new money. Lord Runciman put the 'efficiency expert' firm, Production Engineering, which he had started, in charge and waited for modern methods to take effect. They did take effect, in that after another year or so £80,000 of his money had disappeared.

Robin asked me to see him as in his opinion they were just about to break through into profit. He agreed to think about putting in another £10,000 but changed his mind after consultation. The firm ended up well and truly broke. The Highlands and Islands Board refused to help, saying that after the present firm was liquidated they would perhaps try to pick up the pieces. As a Member of Parliament it appeared to me that this would be disastrous and have a very bad effect on morale. Long years of depression have made people in the Highlands very cynical about new ventures, and this would have been regarded as another nail in the coffin of enterprise.

Happily, at this point we had a white knight. Hugo Brunner, a Liberal candidate, whom I knew, had seen the glass and was intrigued by it. He was interested in putting up some capital if a rescue could be organised. Bill Tawse of the contracting firm, unusually for a contractor, was interested in putting money back where he had made it. Robin Sinclair, too, was now willing to put some of his own money and some of the family trust money towards saving his baby. I was willing to put a little in.

We started to negotiate with Production Engineering who were acting for Lord Runciman. They readily agreed to take 1/- in the pound for their client's shares which was more than they were worth, but fought like tigers for their own fee of £10,000 owing. Eventually we settled for £5,000 to be paid in instalments as and when Caithness Glass could afford it. They eventually settled for even less. My fellow rescuers made it a condition that I became Chairman and we were in business.

It was obvious to me that the sales to tourists had been neglected. In the production of high quality hand-made glass there is always a percentage of seconds which can vary from 50 per cent to 20 per cent. By selling the seconds to tourists at the factory, we actually attained a larger price than the wholesale price of firsts to the shops. We proceeded to exploit this in various ways. We opened a shop out at Inverewe Gardens and a branch in Oban, which had the biggest throughput of tourists in Scotland.

I asked my art student daughter, Diana, to find me a glass engraver who was starving in a garret rather than teach. She came back to me six weeks later and said she could not find a starving engraver but there was a very good art teacher who not only was a top glass engraver but also ran a shop in Lower Largo. This was Colin Terris and when I went to see him we got on extremely well. I said to him, 'We may prostitute your art,' and he replied, 'I have been looking for someone to take commercial advantage of me for years.' He gave up his job and his house and moved north, started a successful glass engraving section, studied paperweight-making and designed the first of the abstract paperweights, now selling for large sums of money to collectors.

The second step was the acquiring of Alistair Mair. A friend of mine, Tommy Hutchison, was a consultant with Urwick Orr. His father had a tremendous reputation when head of Barclay Ross and Hutchison in Aberdeen. He knew everyone and had in fact secured for my father the chance to buy the fine farm of Bent in the Howe of the Mearns. Thinking to myself that son must be like father, I said to Tommy, 'I need a Managing Director for Caithness Glass; he must be doing well, out of at least three generations in Aberdeenshire and educated in Aberdeen. Furthermore, this is on the old boy net. You will be lucky if you get a bottle of whisky!' He laughed, I laughed and we forgot about it.

A month later he telephoned me and said, 'I have the man to your specifications: Aberdeenshire born and bred, educated in Aberdeen, a degree in Engineering and now with Rolls Royce in Scotland but due to go to MIT [Massachusetts Institute of Technology] and thereafter to Derby. He really wants to stay in Scotland.' I met Alistair Mair and after much study of the figures and all sorts of persuasion, he agreed to come. He had a very tough time and I do not think that he would have come if the figures we worked on when engaging him had been correct. Nevertheless, he did and brought the company into profit! After the team of Alistair Mair and Colin Terris got going, we had, of course, many stops, starts and troubles, but we moved into profit and Alistair gave the leadership needed and put in the organisation required.

Alistair left us for a number of reasons, mainly because of the sad illness of his first wife and the fact that he received an offer that we could not match from Royal Worcester. We then had the production manager Matt Young and Colin as joint Managing Directors overseen by an Executive Committee headed by myself. This worked reasonably well. But when we had the chance to get Alistair back, provided we were in a position to expand, I decided to do so.

I found a site in Perth through the good offices of Alistair Duncan Millar who was Convener of the Region at the time. It was on the corner of the main road to the Highlands. We built a factory and showroom and moved the headquarters of the Company down there. Alistair arranged for the factory to be built by the Scottish Development Agency. He organised this with a great deal of skill, using every possible Government and Local Authority aid he could get hold of.

People in Caithness were very suspicious of this move, but it was in my view necessary for the survival of the Company. Although we got both Alistair and Colin to come to Wick originally, Alistair and his wife never really cared enormously for the far north. Colin and Moira did enjoy the north, but they, too, were glad at a later stage to move south. Wick remained as a valuable production base, but one of the measures of the move to Perth is that they are now selling over £1m of seconds through the Perth shop. In the Highlands it is true that with modern communications, business can be done and the success of a local firm manufacturing deep freezes in Caithness is an example of this. But in the main, the difficulty of getting executives to go there, particularly once their children go to college or university, makes it infinitely easier to run the Headquarters in central Scotland.

I was eighteen years as Chairman of the company. I greatly enjoyed it and we brought it from bankruptcy into a strong position, well known all over Great Britain and in many parts of the American continent. My main preoccupation was in getting and keeping top management, but it also entailed a very large amount of decision taking and a constant search for capital to carry out expansion. We had a large number of people interested in looking at investment in Caithness Glass, but it never came to the point of putting in money. Lord Dulverton, who was one of the original shareholders, did in fact lend us £10,000 at a critical stage (when £10,000 was a lot of money). However, being a wise man, and like most multi-millionaires, cautious, he lent the money to me and I lent it to the company. It is the only time I have ever acted as guarantor for a multi-millionaire! Given the history of the company he was, of course, quite right. The main suppliers of capital continued to be myself and Hugo Brunner, the Bank of Scotland and the Highland Board. The Board eventually had a considerable number of shares in the Company, although I saw to it that the Brunner/Tawse/Mackie combination continued to hold a majority.

During the whole time I was Chairman, the success of the Company depended entirely on being able to get rid of seconds at a good price. Eventually we had four main direct selling outlets: Perth, Wick, Oban and a shop at the famous Inverewe Gardens on the west coast. We tried hard to get exports, but in the main, were not particularly successful. The United States was always difficult in spite of spending a great deal of money on visits and promotions.

The development of the paperweight section, both abstract and traditional, made a great impact on sales and on the general raising of esteem in the eyes of the trade and public. One of the best coups we had was when Magnus Magnusson came to us for a trophy for his programme *Mastermind*. We always charged the proper price for the bowl and the BBC always paid it, but in fact we would have paid them handsomely for the privilege of producing the Mastermind Bowl. It was probably the best free advertisement any glass firm ever had.

The main production problem was how to get a high percentage of firsts. This depended on two things. One was the quality of the melted glass and second, of course, the skill of the blowers. We were inclined to go for modern methods of management using these good craftsmen as managers. But on reflection, I think that we should have kept our good blowers as highly skilled artists and craftsmen, giving them the status and remuneration which went with their skill, using them in direct contact with those not so skilled, but always keeping them at their craft whether in blowing, paperweight making or whatever. I think we should have put these top men in charge of teams on the floor, motivating blowers on a piecework system with, of course, a meticulous inspection system. The management on the floor should have been a team business and the blowing teams should have had some responsibility for the quality of the glass.

A simple example in agriculture is the difference between picking potatoes on piecework by the barrel and picking on a daily payment. The breakdown of the digger is greeted with joy by daily paid workers, but on piecework with great irritation and anger, and assistance is offered in any trouble.

One way or another, we got through all our troubles of the day and the firm survived, grew in profitability and general esteem. In 1984 I decided that I had been there too long. Alistair organised a Management buy-out backed by Murray Johnston whom I greatly enjoyed out-manoeuvring. The Company carries on to this day, although no doubt they have a tough time during recessions. Playing my part in the rescue and development of this Company was perhaps as good a bit of work as I ever did, and, as always, getting the right people for the job, in the forms of Alistair Mair and Colin Terris, was the core of our success.

When going round the Caithness and Sutherland constituency with Lindsay, I had always admired the Tongue Hotel, which was a massive former lodge. It was probably the worst hotel in the Highlands. Owned by a supporter of mine, an old man, Mr McKenzie, it was very run down. It had in his father's day been very successfully run as a shooting and fishing hotel, to the high standards of those days. Every time I said to Lindsay, 'I'd like to buy that,' she said, 'Don't be stupid. You think you are clever, but you are not clever enough to run a hotel you know nothing about.' I had to agree.

I then heard that my friend Andrew Lane, who had built up a very successful hotel in Dundee, the Invercarse, had sold out and gone into another business which had been unsuccessful, and wanted to get back into the hotel business. I asked him if he would look at Tongue. He came up with his wife, Jacqui. They reckoned something could be done with it, so I bought the hotel and we formed a little Company, with Andrew and me as Directors along with our wives. We had a great deal of refurbishing to do and redecorated the bedrooms in Victorian style, with roses on the walls. Jacqui was teaching in a College in Newcastle and had to settle the family, some of whom had remained at school there, but she came up and eventually we opened. It was absolutely fascinating for Lindsay and me, but of course Andrew and Jacqui had the work to do. They did so magnificently.

Andrew was a superb hotelier. He loved making a good job. He liked presiding over good food and a beautifully set-out dining room. Within two years Tongue was rated one of the best hotels in the north, not the worst, and we were full all season. Of course, there were troubles. Residents could not get a drink in peace after dinner or even before dinner because the pleasant cocktail bar was filled up with the locals. This was solved by Jacqui taking over the bar herself and we kept it for diners and residents, more or less. Jacqui worked far too hard, however, as she was running the house as well. We also started a snack bar in the stable which opened all summer and made reasonable profits. In those days there was still a lot of traffic around the north, and apart from regulars who came back, the hotel was full all summer. We made constant improvements and were building up the value of the hotel. The profits were small, but we were adding value the whole time.

About 1970 I heard the John o' Groats Hotel was also for sale and bought it in Andrew's absence on holiday. When he came back, I told him what I had done, but said he needn't come in on this if he didn't want to. He thought for a while and said, 'No, no. I will come in with you.' Probably he thought if left to me I would lose money! I started off with great thoughts of development in this most northerly point. John o' Groats did attract large numbers of visitors but they tended to go there simply to say they had been there. After looking at the Pentland Firth, most people turned round and headed south again. Although the John O'Groats pottery and the snack bar did well, that was one hotel which never came up to expectations.

CHAPTER 17

My Last Campaign

I GREATLY ENJOYED the 1970 election campaign in which I fought
Caithness and Sutherland for the third time. We had by this time
got rid of Ian Shaw, the former secretary who I felt had sabotaged us in
1966, and everything worked smoothly in the constituency. An old
friend, Gerald Ritchie, acted as my agent, with tact and efficiency. If he
had been agent in 1966 it would have been more than enough to
reverse the small margin of 64 votes by which I had lost.

Although the Labour Party's image of 'the white heat of technology'
was by then badly tarnished, the Labour candidate who beat me, Bob
MacLennan, turned out to be a very good constituency MP and he had
had four years in which to improve his position. My chances of
regaining the seat were also greatly reduced by the intervention of an
SNP candidate. He was a young music teacher and a good candidate,
who attracted a lot of our previous votes. During these campaigns,
meetings – quite apart from the idea pleasing the electors in the district
who did not attend – were very important. Although you made almost
exactly the same speech at every one, you had to be on your toes,
because the questions afterwards were very much to the point and
sprang in many cases from a deep interest and knowledge of politics.
Poor Lindsay had to be there and appear interested. In the bigger
towns, in Dornoch, Golspie, Helmsdale, Thurso, Wick and Lochinver,
we got a very good turn-out and, if the halls were picked properly,
crowded and enthusiastic meetings. My very first meeting in Brora was
organised by an enthusiastic local Liberal who booked a Nissen hut
capable of seating 300 people. The five who came were a little lost.
This, of course, was another pointer to the amount of education in
political common sense which had to be instilled in my supporters.

However, in the remote area of John O'Groats, one would get fifty
people attending and a really fierce political argument afterwards. The
Tory was a farmer from Banffshire called Hamish Watt, not very
experienced in national politics. His agent slotted in two small country
meetings before his big meeting in Thurso. Unfortunately for him,

both were in the vicinity of John O' Groats. The political passions ran high between Liberals and Labour with only one or two brave Tories in the area. They gave him such hell that he demanded and needed at least two large whiskies before mounting the next platform.

In 1966 they had complained bitterly at John O'Groats because I had to rush off to my final meeting in Wick. So in 1970 I made John O'Groats my last meeting. Coming into a full house, I laid my watch on the table and said, 'Now, I have an appointment for breakfast at 8 o'clock in the morning,' which got the meeting off to a good start and I was able to leave, having exhausted the questioners, at 11.45 p.m. At the eve-of-poll meetings in Thurso and in Wick, the tradition was that the candidates followed each other, with the result that the audience had a political feast of three or four candidates all lecturing them. The final meeting in Wick used to attract well over 1,000 people. Thirty years later, numbers have decreased with the impact of television.

Television in those days didn't play such an important part but it was obviously a great advantage if you were seen on it. During the 1970 campaign, the Scot Nat candidate and I were flown down to Aberdeen to be filmed. We recorded the show and enjoyed the hospitality offered to us. I stuck to whisky, but the Scot Nat, who was a nice fellow, unwisely drank a good deal of beer. On the way back in our small aircraft, the pressure on his bladder became unbearable and he had to take two sick bags, pee into them and sit holding them until we landed. Obviously, I didn't tell this good story until after the Election!

The rise of the Scottish National Party was a phenomenon which greatly excited some people, including Jo and Laura Grimond. Jo Grimond's heart had been unquestionably in Westminster and in Orkney and Shetland. It was not in Edinburgh. It was very difficult to get Jo to talk about a Scottish Parliament, although he would talk happily about devolution. We had in the Party a number of good Liberals who favoured some form of collaboration with the Nats and indeed we were able to have one or two covert election pacts, but not, unfortunately, in Caithness and Sutherland.

Russell Johnston and I were totally against the manoeuvring with the Nats and they lost patience with Jo Grimond, their chairman, referring to him as being like 'the borealis race that flits ere you can point the place'. Great harm was done to us by the journalist Ludovic Kennedy who, in the time that he could spare from investigating the murkier forms of injustice, intervened in Liberal matters. He resigned with the maximum of publicity, but of course never did the logical thing of joining the Scot Nats.

The internecine quarrelling did us great harm, but there is no doubt in my mind that the party would not have accepted any major form of co-operation with the Nats. At that time they included a number of very curious people. John Bannerman, the most fervent Scot in the Party, was never anti-Scottish Nationalism, but certainly was highly suspicious of some of the Nats of that day and was always conscious of the need for a federal system in the United Kingdom. I suppose we should have been able to harness the surge of Scottish feeling instead of the Nats. But the Nationalists did it really by appealing not to a desire for a centre of power and excellence to promote Scotland, but to the anti-English chip on the shoulder which I am afraid many Scots have. I do not regard this sort of campaign as suitable for any Party with the name of Liberal attached to it.

We ran a good campaign in 1970 and right up to the count I was moderately hopeful. The big joint meetings in Thurso and Wick at the end were particularly lively, and I enjoyed them, as I had more experience than the other candidates in dealing with hecklers. It kept the interest going. However the Scottish National Party's intervention saw that MacLennan romped home by a safe margin. Ironically, he is now a good colleague in the Liberal Democrats and has been a very good constituency MP. To say that I, Lindsay and our family were disappointed is an understatement, but political life is like that, and I was certainly lucky in that we had plenty of other things to do.

When I was in the Commons, Lindsay had intended to start a shop in London selling Scottish Crafts and had indeed got premises. By a stroke of fortune the landlord got a better offer and gazumped Lindsay. As I had just been put out of Parliament, this was a great relief. Instead she started a shop in Forfar. She greatly enjoyed this and it gave her a bit of independent income. She also continued her public charity work, particularly for the National Trust for Scotland. She became chairman of the Angus Members Centre and raised a lot of money for the Trust. She enjoyed it and was good at it.

In 1968 our daughter Diana had graduated from Edinburgh School of Art and announced that she would like to get married to a young Edinburgh architect called John Hope, who had used a legacy to buy himself one of the nice old houses in the New Town. I welcomed the chance to organise a wedding at Benshie, but Di wished to get married in a Registry Office. This was going to be very difficult and by a certain amount of manoeuvring, I got them to agree to be married by our minister on the lawn at Benshie. We plunged happily into preparations and of course asked all our friends and Di and John's young friends from Edinburgh. It was exactly the sort of occasion that Lindsay and I loved organising: we had a large marquee erected on the lawn in case of rain, arranged for our friends from the South to be put up, and hoped for good weather. In fact we got the best day that summer in early September. We proceeded from the house and John Skinner made a very good job of marrying the pair, looking out over the beautiful and fertile Howe of Strathmore. As soon as the ceremony was over, I arranged that the waitresses would be waiting with trays of drink in the tent and, sure enough, I waved my handkerchief and they poured out to quench the thirst of the guests.

We had the Forfar Brass Band in attendance, who were, at the outset, competent and sober. The whole thing worked like a dream. The band played beautifully. But towards the end of the afternoon they became a little repetitive and indeed, going out of the small gate on the way home, had some trouble with the instruments.

Everyone was in great fettle. The toast to the bride and groom was proposed by a friend, Margaret Thorpe, but the toast of the day was a toast to the parents of the bride proposed by my old friend George Raeburn. He obviously had done a lot of work and was, of course, extremely funny about me and nice about Lindsay and, as it was largely a Mackie wedding, his jokes and references went down extremely well. Everyone said it was the best speech they had ever heard at a wedding. I replied very shortly, knowing that I had no hope of competing with this masterpiece.

The catering was done by Goodfellow and Steven from Dundee, David Goodfellow being a friend of ours. After the wedding on the lawn was over and we were tidying up, I saw David Goodfellow emerge from the back regions of the tent, whereupon I produced more champagne. I really was extremely grateful to him and I might have known that the thing would not have worked so perfectly had it not been for the presence of the boss behind the scenes. I took this as a great compliment and Lindsay and I were very grateful. We let off balloons over the valley and eventually we got one back from Aberdeenshire. It must have gone out to sea and come back, but it won the prize. We had one or two set-piece photos, but a good photographer from Montrose simply moved about taking pictures of people informally, including one of a young lady who is now a graduate of a distinguished university but who was then aged two, bent double and looking through her legs backwards. She is Ben Coutts' eldest daughter and, funnily enough, she is still quite amused when we tell this story.

Eventually we saw the bride and groom away to a honeymoon in an ill-equipped cottage on the west coast, with a hip bath on top of the Mini! The dance was a great success and Lindsay and I retired, pleased with the wedding, but much poorer. Di and John have now been married for over thirty years and the result of the union is four grand-daughters of whom I am extremely fond and proud.

Lindsay, our eldest daughter, and Jeannie, our youngest, both married some years later in London, both to able journalists, Alan Rusbridger and David Leigh. After the two excellent and enjoyable London weddings were over, we thought it safe to expose the new husbands to the full force of a Mackie gathering, and held a buffet dance (mostly reels) in Kirriemuir Town Hall. I thought a good feature would be suckling pig, so four piglets were arranged on a giant ashet. The women all said, 'Oh, the poor things,' but then swiftly said, 'I'll have that bit!' It was a good party and Alan and David braved the reels and lived on. I now have three further grand-daughters, Hannah from Jeannie and David, and Tibby and Lizzie Lindsay from Alan and Lindsay – and I am delighted with them all.

CHAPTER 18

The House of Lords

B Y 1974 I HAD BEEN out of politics for nearly four years and the old
poison was working on me. In the first '74 election in February, I
decided that I must get in the fray and rang David Steel to see if he
could do with some help. He accepted gratefully. I went down to the
Borders to find him somewhat despondent but fighting hard. I think I
succeeded in cheering him up a little and plunged happily into the old
routine. David won the election fairly narrowly, but the main thing was
that he did actually win. He was at the time Chief Whip. He went back
to tell Jeremy Thorpe that 'we must get George Mackie back into
politics'. He suggested that at the first chance of a life peerage I should
be the one to get it. Jeremy simply loved playing the part of the
disposer of honours (not that one can blame him for this). I was seated
in my office at Caithness Glass one day when I had a rather excited call
from him offering to put me up for the peerage. I hesitated for about a
tenth of a second and then, as we say about bargains in farming, 'bit his
hand off'.

Indeed everyone around seemed to be pleased; one not particularly
close friend telephoned at 6.30 a.m. having got her newspaper,
absolutely delighted. The men on the farm were pleased, as were all
our friends, which greatly added to our own pleasure. We all went to
London for my introduction to the House and had a good party. The
antique ceremony was totally out-dated and amusing, but I liked it.
Preceded by the Herald sweating in his glorious tunic, you march in,
bow at various points, kneel to the Lord Chancellor with your paper,
take the oath and then proceed to a back seat in order for you and your
two sponsors to take off your hats and bow three times to the Lord
Chancellor. The degree of co-ordination of the hat-taking-off is noted
by the older members. Then you march up, again bowing every ten
steps, and the new peer shakes hands with the Lord Chancellor. At this
point there is either a loud growl of 'Hear, hear' or a muted growl of
'Hear, hear', according to the popularity of the new peer.

There is no doubt that in the UK people like Lords and also like being Lords, although the whole set up is an anachronism. The respect and curiosity excited in many members of the community, in Europe and at home, is really rather amusing. If one realises that one is really an unpaid senator, one can enjoy it.

Getting a peerage gave at least as much pleasure to Lindsay as it did to me. She liked her title and deserved it. My daughters Lindsay, Diana and Jeannie were pleased for their parents. They were rather embarrassed in front of their left-wing friends, but endured it happily. I asked Lindsay if we should buy a London flat, having rented one when I was in the Commons. Her reply was simple – 'I like staying in the Farmers Club. I don't want to spend my time when I come to London changing your dirty sheets.' It was sensible and I continue staying there or in the RAF Club when in London.

I had also been a Country Member of the Garrick since 1966 owing to a St David's Day party with Hugh Griffiths, the Welsh actor, and Emlyn Hooson, the Liberal MP for Montgomery. I was put up by Emlyn and seconded by Hugh Griffiths who saw to it that my page in the aspiring members' book was filled up by the famous – either by request or, I suspect, by forgery. I was elected in a matter of months as against today's waiting list of some years.

At the House of Lords, the attendants are headed by the door-keepers, who are highly efficient; they are all hand picked from non-commissioned officers of the various forces and most of them look much more impressive than the peers. Like the regular policemen, they have got to be highly intelligent as they have to memorise the faces of at least three or four hundred peers. They do it extraordinarily well.

I liked the Lords and quickly settled down to the work. I was delighted when on my first day as a peer I went into tea and found that everyone closed up together cross bench Labour/Liberal/Tory instead of the segregation of a severe sort that takes place in the House of Commons dining-room. The atmosphere in the Chamber is more relaxed and, on the whole, better than in the Commons, and infinitely less charged with party antagonism – although I sometimes think we could do with a little more bite and less politeness. The standard of speech is probably on average higher than in the Commons, although the hereditary peers make a fairly poor showing, despite one or two excellent ones. I have never understood why the Tory Government did not use their powers to create more really competent Ministers in the Lords, such as Russell Sanderson. He was Minister of State at the

Scottish Office, a Scottish businessman from the Borders, who knew the basic problems of Scotland and was an excellent Minister who used his own initiative. He then gave up his job to chair the Tory Party in Scotland to the great detriment of the quality of the Scottish Ministers.

The young hereditary peers the Tories love to put in as spokesmen are not, with the odd exception, up to the job, although they are amiable and able to read a brief. The Special Committees of the House of Lords are, in my view, of better quality than the Committees of the Commons, because party politics play little part and in a specialist field, they produce work of great value. For example, the EEC Scrutiny Committee's Reports are studied with great care in Brussels and members of the Commission have told me that the House of Lords Reports are the most valuable that they receive from outside sources.

I would not myself like to see the House of Lords as an elected Second Chamber. I think nomination is very valuable and it is also very cheap. The allowances on a daily basis are quite adequate if, for example, you stay in a Club, but they are certainly not over generous. I have investigated the cost to firms of fairly junior executives on a visit to London and the cost is much higher than the expenses paid to peers. I certainly do not complain about the expenses, in that, although it sometimes costs me more, this is due to my liking for a good dinner and the fact that I quite often entertain colleagues from Europe and elsewhere to lunch or dinner in the House.

After accepting (grabbing!) a peerage, it was necessary to tidy my affairs in Caithness. I was heavily involved in hotels, glass, cheese making, building and potteries and in property. 1974 was a year of financial crisis and I was heavily over borrowed. The hotels, particularly Tongue, were holding their value and we tried to raise the cash for Andrew and Jacqui to take on Tongue on their own, but this was not possible. We then had a good offer from Highland Hotels for Tongue and accepted it.

I wanted to sell John O' Groats straight away but Andrew was afraid that it would not realise its full value, so he and Jacqui took it on. We liquidated our joint company, which gave us £10,000 each of capital profit. Andrew later sold John O' Groats and moved to manage the Buchanan Arms at Drymen for Highland Hotels, bringing it back to its old glory in a short time. I wound up Caithness Cheese a year too late, lost my loans to the Company and had to pay the Bank £30,000 on my guarantee. This took all the profit and the original capital I had had in

Tongue Hotel. A builder's business in which I was involved was easy and left a little profit, while Caithness Glass took on the potteries, selling the John O' Groats one at a good profit. I was left with a spectacular house on the cliff at Whaligoe, which I took nearly three years to sell while paying high interest rates. I should have realised that the first loss is the best one: Caithness Glass was being run successfully and continued to contribute significantly to employment in Caithness.

My return to active politics in 1974 was not altogether welcomed by the Scottish Liberal Party. In the previous four years, they had progressed to their own way of working under Russell Johnston and Lady Bannerman. Ray Bannerman did a tremendous job and was a little reluctant to give up. However, by 1976 she decided to retire and I put up for the presidency. The party conference occurred at the same time as the Jeremy Thorpe story broke, with the allegations about a homosexual relationship with an unstable young man, Norman Scott, whom Jeremy was eventually – following a sensational trial at the Old Bailey – acquitted of conspiring to murder.

I made no secret of the fact that I thought Jeremy should go. This was deeply unpopular with the loyal Scottish troops. An Edinburgh Town Councillor called Smith put up against me as President and it became apparent at the conference that I was totally out of favour. Jeremy came up to speak, and received a standing ovation when he came in, and a standing ovation after he spoke. Obviously, I did not take part. As a result, I was thoroughly beaten by Smith who became President. I was a little perturbed by this, not because I had been beaten, but because of the lack of common sense in the Party.

However, it could not have mattered less, as I had my new and interesting work in the House of Lords. It was a very curious period. I had thought that, after our successes in 1964 and indeed in 1966, we would get a flood of good people as candidates. It did not materialise. I find this a little curious, in that in 1959 and 1964 we got a very large number of good young candidates, and indeed middle-aged people standing. I can only imagine that the fact that we did not make power pushed normally Liberal inclined people into the Labour Party or indeed to join the few Liberal minded people in the Tory Party. The rise of the SNP also attracted a lot of good people. The splitting of the Scottish vote between the Liberal Democrats and the SNP is harmful to progress.

I eventually became President in the 1980s. But prior to that, the first election to the European Parliament took place in 1979 and in order to help the Party, I agreed to stand in the North East Scotland constituency, which was good Mackie territory. I didn't wish to be elected, but merely to make a decent showing for the Liberal Party. A number of friends rallied round and the family in Aberdeenshire was mobilised. Of course I realised we could never cover the enormous area with a conventional campaign. The order of the day was to be seen and heard in every corner. We therefore organised that everywhere I went we had a band of supporters, highly decorated vehicles and plenty of loudspeakers. From being an exercise, it developed into a real campaign, and I wanted to win. Unfortunately, Headquarters made a mess of my television appearances by scheduling two inside the constituency, which was against the rules. All it needed was to appear for the broadcast outside your own area and all would watch legally and happily. It was too late to change and I lost the chance to impress on the Box. In spite of this, I came a decent second to the Tory, Jim Provan, who made a good Euro MP for the area. Moreover, it was the most improved result for the Liberals in Scotland. The figures were: Provan, James – Conservative – 51,930; Lord Mackie of Benshie – Liberal – 38,416; Clyne, D. – Labour – 38,139; Bell, C – SNP – 28,886.

In 1981 I was elected Rector of Dundee University, following Clement Freud. I was elected by a decent margin and was pulled over the Tay Bridge and back in an open carriage by my supporters. I was pleased with this honour and quite soon realised what my role should be. The governing body of the University was the Court, presided over by the Principal, Adam Neville, and consisting of various senior members of staff and representatives of public bodies in the area. As my Assessor, I was fortunate in getting Kathleen Smith, who had been Freud's Assessor. She was a good Liberal, and knew the ropes. I got on well with Adam Neville and his wife, Mary, and many members of the Court.

Adam was able but impulsive: a little bit of doggerel amused him and Mary:

> There was a professor called Neville
> A handsome, moustachioed devil
> He had a good fairy
> Aptly named Mary
> Who kept him remarkably level.

The Court was obviously mainly on the students' side and I taught that generation of students that if you didn't alienate the outside members, they would be sympathetic to any reasonably put request. During my time we never lost a case in the Court of the University. I greatly enjoyed my time as Rector and was gratified when I was awarded an honorary degree. The University of Dundee has gone from strength to strength in research and popularity and has done the City of Dundee much good.

In 1983 we had a successful General Election with two new MPs, Malcolm Bruce and Archie Kirkwood, elected. We had an Executive Meeting where the main point was to consume a bottle of whisky, then took the successful candidates to dinner which was, of course, cheerful and rather liquid. I then took them to Waverley Station in Edinburgh where they took the night train. I myself was flying down the next day. I had another glass of port and set off for home in cheerful mood. I was driving my wife's car which was a hotted up Ford Escort. I was driving cheerfully along the road towards Perth at what I thought was a reasonable speed, but turned out to be 90 m.p.h., when I saw a flashing blue light behind me. Along came the police and we had a chat about the excellence of my wife's car, how fast it would go, and it was all very amiable and then, of course, they charged me. They did not breathalyse me, for which I suppose I should be thankful. This cost me £40 and the policemen were quite tickled – one of them said he had never booked a Lord before!

Ten years later I was coming home from the airport – this time, happily, totally without drink in me, late at night. I got through Coupar Angus and thought that as there was nothing behind, I would speed up. This I did, when suddenly, again flashing blue lights behind me – the policemen had been lurking in a lay-by. Again, we had a very pleasant chat and they then asked me for my name. I gave my name as was on my licence – George Y. Mackie, then they asked my occupation. I wondered if I would say retired and thought I should better be honest and said 'Peer of the Realm', whereupon there was a loud shout from one of the bobbies, 'I kent it. I kent it. I booked you ten years ago driving your wife's car!' We had another long chat and I asked them not to make a habit of it. This one cost me another £40.

One of the great differences between life in the Lords and the Commons is that you are no longer burdened by an enormous amount of constituency work. The mail bag of MPs nowadays is quite ridiculous and much of their time is spent as a sort of welfare officer for complaints which should really be dealt with at local government level. It is true that a good secretary can handle many of these matters and pass them to the correct channel, but nevertheless it involves the Member of Parliament in a great deal of time, which could be better spent on more important matters. It is absolutely essential that an MP is in close touch with the daily lives of his constituents, but it has gone too far, and many of them are in the position of being unable to see the wood for the trees.

However, in 1980 I had a letter from a friend, Colonel David Lloyd-Jones. He said that a foolish young man, John Lawlor, who had been one of his battalion, had been persuaded to go to Angola in a group of mercenaries. These young men had been seduced by letters on bogus official paper to think that this was a straightforward organisation – instead of which it was purely a financial device for the benefit of the recruiter. They were captured. The leaders were shot and the remainder had been sentenced to terms of 24 years imprisonment, under extremely poor conditions. They had been there for a number of years and certainly had been punished enough. Efforts were being made by various people to persuade the Angolan authorities to release them, without much success.

In October 1976 an approach had been made to the Papal representative in Angola. In 1977, Mrs Lawlor was put in touch with Julian Critchley, the MP for Aldershot, and in July 1977 Mrs Lawlor was invited by David Owen, then Foreign Secretary, to 'wait and see'. In 1978 there were curious efforts by unknown sources to try 'springing' the mercenaries. In 1978 a BBC television programme was stopped by the Foreign Office at the last minute. In April 1978 our Consul Representative was granted permission to see the mercenaries. In June 1978 Brendan Williams MP took an interest. In July Dr Owen stated that Mr Flynn, the Consul Representative, had seen the mercenaries and thought they were in reasonable health. By 1980 the mercenaries' health appeared to be deteriorating.

In November 1982 I thought we ought to get a small committee together in order to bring influence to bear on the Foreign Office. We had a meeting of interested people, who included such diverse sorts as Harvey Proctor MP, Sir Derek Walker-Smith MP, Monsignor Bruce Kent of the Campaign for Nuclear Disarmament, Bill Homewood MP, a representative of Sir Brandon Rhys-Williams, and myself. It was obvious that we should get Derek Walker-Smith, as a senior Tory MP, to be our main representative, and he agreed that he would try to see the Foreign Secretary. Harvey Proctor reported that he had met the Angolan chargé d'affaires in Brussels and I reported I had found a source of money for travel, if the committee thought it was necessary. Monsignor Bruce Kent reported that he had delegated or persuaded the Catholic Bishop Victor Guazzelli, a fluent Portuguese speaker, to go to Angola if necessary.

A great deal of credit for their eventual release must go to our new Ambassador, whom we saw before he left to take up his job. He approached the whole thing with new vigour and I think that this in itself had a great effect in securing the release. The previous Ambassador had been there for some time and had got rather discouraged by the non-success of his efforts. On 5 March 1983 I had a letter from Malcolm Rifkind, the Foreign Secretary, saying that seven British prisoners had been released by the end of February. The prisoners had unanimously asked our ambassador in Luanda that no-one should be told, including their families, until their plane was airborne and well on its way. The Foreign Office, with great care, made the men sign an agreement that they would repay the £750 that it cost to send them home.

We did try to stop the recruitment of mercenaries, but, of course, that proved impossible and indeed, as long as mercenaries realise the risks they are taking, they are entitled to serve anywhere they wish. Bruce Kent told me that he had been to see the families he was interested in and had seen their great joy at the reunion. I myself never met John Lawlor, but I had a letter from him and Christmas cards for a number of years afterwards. It is seldom that one gets any credit for effort, but he and his family were grateful and said so.

In a typical day at the Lords, I would stay in the Farmers Club, which is just off Whitehall and is only a leisurely ten minutes walk away. I normally read the papers there, with a politician's interest, and get down to the House about 10 o'clock. I pick up my mail at the Liberal Whip's Office, go past the Printed Paper Office, pick up Hansard and the Order Paper, then proceed to my own office. This is a somewhat grandiose name for my desk in a room which I share with ten other Liberal Peers. I read Hansard, answer my mail, prepare for any questions I wish to come in on in the afternoon, and catch up on the large amount of reading I feel obliged to do. This is on a day when I have no Committee to attend.

For many years I was on the busiest of the House of Lords EEC Scrutiny Sub Committees. This was Sub Committee D which looked into proposed agricultural legislation. This committee met on Wednesday at 10.30 a.m. and frequently went on to one o'clock. I think we produced some valuable reports, on both fishing and agriculture. One, which I chaired, was on the olive oil industry, which is absolutely fraught with difficulties, both social and economic. Industry support was totally open to fraud. In Italy in particular, one had very curious examples of discrepancies between the amount paid out and the amount of olive oil marketed. I proposed to cut through the complicated mass of subsidies by simply paying a subsidy, according to area, on each olive tree. They could be checked by aerial photography. The subsidy would be paid whether the tree was harvested or not and this in itself would probably cure the surplus problem. I understand the report was greatly liked and admired by members of the Commission, but they thought it was far too practical to put into operation and would give rise to serious criticism. It certainly would have cost a great deal less, would have given the social support necessary in many olive growing areas and would not have been subject to fraud.

After my committee sessions, I would normally go down to the members' dining room and have lunch. It is always taken at a long table where happily, unlike the Commons, all parties sit together. After lunch, further study of the newspapers is taken in one of the comfortable leather armchairs in the House of Lords library (which in many cases involves a post luncheon snooze). Prayers are at 2.30 p.m. and after Prayers we have Question Time. Oral questions in the House of Lords are entirely different to Question Time in the Commons. We have 30 minutes for four questions, which means that there is a genuine debate on each question rather than the machine gunfire attitude of the Commons, with smart-alec answers and questions. I regard this as a valuable time when many matters of real interest to the public are ventilated – often with good effect on the Minister involved.

Question Time can often be quite amusing. For example, my car was clamped outside the Farmers Club, where I had left it for six minutes while taking in my luggage. I raised the matter 'in the public interest' and when I said this, there was a roar of laughter, but in fact the questioning that followed revealed that the 'pack' actually had a target to aim for and were more or less paid on results.

After Question Time we go to the business of the day, which on a Wednesday may be one or two timed debates selected from individual members by ballot or put down by the parties when it is their day. These debates are often very useful for speeches may be limited to eight minutes or even less. It concentrates the mind wonderfully. On other days, Committees and Second Readings are taken. The Second Reading debate on a controversial subject may last until after midnight. On Committee days the content of a bill is examined, clause by clause, and amendments are put down both by the Opposition and the Government to improve the bill. No amendment should actually be a wrecking amendment, but it may substantially alter the effect of the clause on the public. The Committee stage of a bill may go on into the early hours of the morning.

If speaking in any debate or taking part in Committee, of course one has to stay there the whole time, although in the Second Reading one can have a break after the speech succeeding one's own and before the wind up of the debate. If I am not either Duty Peer or speaking, then I would normally have a decent dinner in the Commons at the Liberal table where peers who have been members of the Commons can go. I find this very congenial and it keeps a very useful contact between the two Houses. It is a long day but nearly always interesting. There are, however, one or two peers who are such blethers, I would happily shoot them!

I know that I am very lucky to be there, taking part in the political life of the country, and enjoying myself. The House of Lords has now been altered – I wouldn't say reformed – and a bonny mess the Leader of the House and the Lord Chancellor have made of it. The Government had the ultimate weapon; with the Parliament Act in February 2000, they could have sacked every hereditary peer and the Tory Party would have been reduced to a minority group. But they were out-manoeuvred by the Lord Cranborne and the former Tory Speaker of the House of Commons, Lord Weatherill. So anxious were the Government to get their legislation through that the Tory Party, which was allotted 42 hereditary peers, can count on over 80 hereditary votes in a crucial division, thanks to 'independent' votes. I eventually came off the front bench and only spoke in the chamber when I was interested and had some knowledge of the subject, or if I got the opportunity to make a crack at the Government or the Opposition.

As a member of Sub Committee D of the European Committee I

had plenty of opportunity to use my experience. It is a combination of the Agricultural Committee and the Environmental Committee – the practical agricultural view and the more emotional (but still important) supporters of biodiversity in Government legislation. The subjects vary from food safety to sustainability to fishing policy – all problems which need to have a European and worldwide focus. They are complex issues and need work and understanding. Jo Grimond used to call the House of Lords 'The Old Folk's Home'. But no one ever dies there. You are not allowed to die in the Palace of Westminster. I have known several people collapse, but it has always been alleged that they were taken to hospital, and died on the way. A curious tradition. But it is also a fact that because life continues to be interesting, people do last a long time in the House of Lords. Manny Shinwell was making speeches when he was over 100 and we had Douglas Houghton at well over 90 putting forward with clarity and precision Bills on his great passion which was animal welfare. I personally have no desire or hope to be doing this. I am firmly of the view that we should all have a retiring age of perhaps 75. Yet, although I am now in my 80s and no doubt signs of age are there, I still enjoy the House. I think I have been useful for the Liberal Party, and I make no bones about saying that I greatly enjoy being a peer. The serious advantage is the ability to do interesting work as long as you are able.

CHAPTER 19

A Visit to China

MY LINKS TO China first began in early 1978. I was sitting on the bench during a dull debate in the House of Lords when I was called out to speak to Hervey Rhodes – Lord Rhodes of Saddleworth. He was a man I admired greatly. A textile worker, he was bred off a very able family of weavers, steeped in the musical tradition of Yorkshire and Lancashire. He told me that his grandfather could take an operatic score and transcribe it straight on to paper for a brass band. He went to Canada, but returned to join the Forces on the outbreak of the First War. He served in the King's Own Royal Lancs and transferred to the RFC. There he became an Observer and was commissioned. He gained a great reputation with two Distinguished Flying Crosses, but was shot down and badly wounded on a special mission in September 1918. He spent two years in hospital and when he came out, he still had to dress his wounds every day until the discovery of penicillin.

He installed two or three looms in a shed he built himself and started manufacturing. By the outbreak of the Second War he had one of the most modern factories in the north of England. He won a Labour seat in a by-election in 1945, becoming Trade Minister in the Attlee Government. He was made a Knight of the Garter in 1972 and as a Yorkshireman became Lord Lieutenant of Lancashire. At the age of 80, he went on an Inter-Parliamentary Union delegation to South America and had put in a very, very able Report. This was the man who wanted to see me, so you can imagine I went out immediately. He said, 'Would thee [he occasionally used the old Yorkshire form] like to join a delegation I am taking to China?' I pulled out my diary and I said, 'When?' I then shut the diary and said, 'It does not matter when. I will come.'

China was just recovering from the appalling mess of the Cultural Revolution. The Foreign Office approved, but Hervey Rhodes picked his own delegation and found the money from his industrial friends, who were far seeing enough to back this venture. I was to be the 'expert' on agriculture and the other members were Labour MP Ben Ford, Tory MP Hal Miller, Lord Fulton and Lord Bowden, Laurie Pavitt MP, John Biffen MP, Peter Temple-Morris MP and Bryan Gould MP. All this was done by Hervey himself, at the age of 83, crippled though he was with his war wounds.

We landed in Hong Kong after a 17-hour flight and went to the Mandarin Hotel, one of the best I have ever stayed in. At an exhibition of Chinese art, they showed us a bowl of very reasonable pottery which had been found to be 6,000 years old. This was a good start for anybody visiting China, as one has to realise the age of the civilisation before one can appreciate the present.

The agriculture in the New Territories was very intensive and very well done. We walked over the famous bridge between the New Territories and Communist China and, after a number of formalities, got on the train to Canton. We were very struck by the Victorian railway carriages – each one kept spotlessly clean by a stewardess who also served us tea. The seat backs had antimacassars. The litter in some parts of the Hong Kong New Territories was quite appalling, but as we passed into China we immediately saw a terrific difference in the tidiness of the roads and indeed the fields. The neatness of the cultivation and the good care of the land pleased me enormously. It was obviously mainly done by hand labour, though we saw buffalos ploughing.

We were well received in Canton and flew on in an old Russian aircraft to Peking. We were charmingly waited on by nice stewardesses, who served us fresh orange juice poured out of a kettle, from which afterwards they gave us tea. On arrival in Peking, we were put up in the very comfortable Peking Hotel. I think you first realise that there are 1,000 million Chinese when you see them coming towards you on bicycles. In 1978 they all wore Mao tunics and it presented rather a drab picture, but we were in the middle of a society where if you were privileged, you were very privileged. The hierarchical situation was strictly adhered to and happily they thought Lords were more important than members of the Commons. Hervey Rhodes and Hal Miller were ushered into a black limo with curtains, and the rest of us were put in pairs in four other cars – and we surged through the streets, crossing crossroads with abandon. We proceeded to look at various communes, seeing how intensively the land could be farmed with lots of labour, and how the Chinese were developing self-governing bodies who did all sorts of things. They had factories, hospitals, schools – all run by the commune. They were never free from central direction, but the amount of bureaucratic interference even then was getting much less.

The ceremonial for meeting the top brass was fixed and quite impressive. We were to meet Number Four in the hierarchy in the Great Hall of the People. Ushered into an ante-room, we were joined by the great man and his satellites and acolytes. Then we lined up for photographs and went into the Conference Room, where we sat in a circle with the great man and Hervey in the centre. We were then served tea and the conference began. Everything was interpreted, though in many cases we knew that the official speaking was a fluent English speaker. Number Four and Hervey were both limping. The Chinese said to Hervey, 'Why do you limp?' Hervey said, 'War wounds.' He slapped his thigh and said, 'Me too. War wounds!' This certainly made a bond between them. Their main political thrust was to ensure that we saw the danger of Russia, and wherever we went we got the same line. They could not say enough in condemnation of Russian imperialism. We liked, as everyone does, the ordinary Chinese. Our interpreters were intelligent and friendly, although, at this time, well within the bounds of discretion.

Our banquet was a very formal occasion round a large round table with course after course of delicious Chinese food – none of which the ordinary Chinese could ever hope to eat. The hosts would pick up the delicacies with special chopsticks and place them on your plate. We also had a series of toasts, mostly drunk in a very sweet and strong liqueur called 'My Tie' (actually Mai Tai). They always started quite early and finished promptly at 8.30 p.m. when I assumed that our hosts went off to have a little home life.

We went to Nanking and visited a factory there with a very competent manager. He told us the terrible difficulties they had during the Cultural Revolution when senior managers were beaten by mobs of Red Guards, in some cases beaten to death and in others sent to work on the land. Production was constantly interrupted. In Shanghai we went to a very good hospital where we were shown round by two obviously very high level medics of great ability, who said that the one thing they would never allow in China again was the Cultural Revolution's chaos. They said it with enormous feeling and bitterness and one could see that it must have been pure hell for able people trying to do their jobs. At one university as we looked at a reading room full of students hard at work, the librarian told us, again with great bitterness, that during the Cultural Revolution there might have been one student there and the rest of them would be roaming the countryside beating honest men who were trying to do their jobs. It is quite apparent that the Cultural Revolution produced a whole generation who missed their education and who must regret that period to the end of their days. All sorts of reasons are now produced for Mao's ordering the break-up of the society he had created. My theory (after five minutes in China) is that as he got older he saw a renewed type of Mandarin running this vast country. He resented and feared the rise of the technocrats, and indeed all the rising class of political leaders, and decided that chaos was preferable to this sort of order. It was mad and set China back for years.

We were always taken to the best schools, but they were a delight to see. The receptions were staged, but were very charming. The education appeared to me to be exactly like the one I received in the village school in Aberdeenshire sixty years earlier. They learned by rote in the same way as I remember being taught to recite the Shorter Catechism and multiplication tables. The Chinese appeared to be very good students and there is no doubt that an educated class was being produced.

In the hospital in Shanghai we were shown an operation on the throat done with no other anaesthetic than acupuncture. It certainly looked impressive. Our hosts said they used it alongside modern medicine, and quite often the acupuncture was more effective. In many places we went to on this first tour we were curiosities, in that not even Russians had been common since the Great Split. Indeed when we were being shown round a temple near Nanking, getting privileged entrance to the shrines in front of the native Chinese, two young women were sitting chatting and they suddenly looked up and saw me. I must have appeared like a monster because they burst into a fit of giggles and put their hands up to their mouths to restrain their mirth.

That first trip was certainly the most exciting and revealing. But the people were clad in the uniform of dull Mao tunics – male and female – and no one came up to us in the street to try out their English. When we visited places like the Forbidden City, our guides would push the native Chinese out of the way in order that we should have priority. The people in the hotel and porters would not take tips and the standard of service – certainly in the good official hotels – was good. An American engineer we met who had worked all over the world said to us with great cynicism, 'Well, they won't take tips just now, but I reckon we will corrupt them within a couple of years.'

This proved to be true. But we came out there that first trip perfectly certain that we were seeing an awakening giant in industrial power. I was also of the opinion that the brutal centralisation and reorganisation of the old corrupt China of the War Lords and the Kuomintang could only have been done by a strong central authority. Lord Rhodes took another delegation of which I was a member in 1979, 15 months later, and another in 1981. We saw big changes. The most noticeable was the introduction of colour and variety in the clothes, particularly of the women. The drab tunics were thrown away in favour of more feminine clothes. By 1981, people were not afraid to come up to you in the street in order to practise their English and indeed to discuss the political situation. In 1981, I flew out to a Joint Enterprise just over the Hong Kong border. It was a dairy farm, selling the milk in Hong Kong, and a quail farm. The quails appeared to withstand appalling conditions and I was told they laid 22 eggs a month, they did not eat a great deal of food and the eggs sold at twice the price of a hen's egg. I intended to start a quail farm in Scotland, but I was waylaid – but I may still do so.

The dairy enterprise used all the techniques of Western agriculture, although they also used a great deal of labour. The local Chinese happily accepted capitalist techniques as the wages, though low, were far in advance of those paid by state enterprises. The process of expansion and production in China is now going at breakneck speed. It will be most interesting to see if strong political control will persist. The considerable achievements of the Communist government since 1949 have been made by total repression. The subjugation of 1,000 million people could only have been carried out with brutal methods. The village meetings to see that everyone was thinking correctly, the compulsory abortions in order to keep down the rise in population and the many executions obviously made China an intolerable place in which to live – witness the number of people who flocked into Hong Kong risking their lives to get there.

We enjoyed Hong Kong and got this extraordinary feeling of excitement and bustle which I had got in Manhattan forty years earlier. On the last two visits the peers in our party stayed at Government House, our hosts being the Governor, Sir John MacLehose, and Lady

MacLehose. Sir John had a deep understanding of the Chinese. It appears to me that his wise advice was ignored and later replaced by confrontational attitudes. All old China hands tell me that you can be as tough as you like with the Chinese in private dealings, but anything that appears to make them lose face is immediately followed by total opposition. The most frightening example of this was the Tiananmen Square uprising that took place during the visit of Gorbachev to Peking, thereby causing a terrific loss of face and the resultant brutal reaction. The subsequent massacre was a disaster not only because of the deaths of innocent people, but because it stopped the progress towards some political freedom which the old guard were beginning to tolerate.

In a hotel in China, in Chanking close to the Himalayas in 1981, I had a moment I will never forget. We had spent the day inspecting agriculture on the slopes, and the very creditable local measures to bring water. We saw peasants bring pigs to market on the back of their bicycles, tied up so that they appeared to like it and were contented. It certainly brought to mind the expression 'hog tied'.

That night we were sitting at a table with John Hunt, the conqueror of Everest, who was also on the delegation. A colleague and I on our parliamentary delegation started quizzing him on the detail of the first ascent of the mountain. The final assault was made together by the New Zealander, Edmund Hillary, and the experienced Sherpa Tenzing. John said that he considered it had been a mistake to team up climbers on the basis of their past experience, and he had determined to wait until they got on to the Himalayan slopes. There, it became obvious to him very early that Hillary and Tenzing made a wonderful team.

Then, just as he said this, a hand fell on John's shoulder in our hotel. He looked up and sprang to his feet and embraced the newcomer. This was Tenzing himself! He was staying in the hotel for one night taking a party of Americans to Tibet. Tenzing and Hunt, of course, spent the rest of the evening together. It was a most extraordinary, dramatic moment.

CHAPTER 20

The Inter Parliamentary Union

IN THE LORDS you can pursue your interests without the distraction of constituency work. Also, of course, the Whips are unable to exert the pressures usual in the Commons and indeed I do not think they always wish to. I joined the Inter Parliamentary Union and took a great interest in this very important organisation. It was started one hundred years ago by an Englishman and a Frenchman. Any country that has a parliament, however ineffective, can become a member. The only regimes really excluded are military dictatorships. This may seem ridiculous, but of course the mingling with genuine parliamentarians does make a difference to members who come from countries where the Members of Parliament are puppets of the Government. It assists in progress to proper parliamentary democracy. In Britain we entertain delegations from all over the world, showing our parliamentary procedure and something of life in Britain. We in turn send delegations to places as far removed as Seoul and South America. The IPU has played its part, for example in improving relations between Britain and Argentina.

Two annual conferences are also held in various countries. Spouses are welcome at the member's expense and indeed very useful. I was fortunate enough to be selected for a number of conferences – perhaps the most interesting one was in Mexico. Lindsay accompanied me. I was taken about by a young Mexican veterinary officer and in this way I learned a great deal about the countryside and the problems. On one of these trips, we came across a roadside stall. My companion said, 'I must eat something,' but when I made to join him he waved me back and said, 'Without any doubt, you will have tummy trouble if you eat. My stomach is used to it, but you will have trouble!' I had to stay and watch him eat the most delicious chillies and other things cooked over a charcoal stove, with hunger gnawing at my insides. He was, of course, right.

I will not pretend that these trips were not most enjoyable. People talk of MPs getting freebies or junketing and it is certainly true that we were entertained extraordinarily well. But we made friendships with people from all over the world which must be of value. Of course, mistakes were made. One conference in Lagos was appallingly badly organised. But even there I made a lasting friendship with a Senator, Oneabo Obi, who was a lawyer, a member of Gray's Inn. We still meet. I was able to study improvement schemes in the north of the country by flying up to Kano for a day (at my own expense). One of the tragedies of Nigeria is that with the oil revenue, they allowed their agriculture to collapse in favour of importing food, a source of corruption in itself and which has driven people off the land into the cities, often to become part of a criminal society.

In March 1985 a conference was held in Togo. This was a mistake. The President was an absolute dictator and the country exhibited all the worst features of an African state. At our hotel, we found many delegates had had their reservations cancelled because the President was holding a meeting of the Heads of West African states. He had arranged it for the same time as the IPU Conference, the presence of which he had originally eagerly canvassed. The pantomime in the hotel with military guards flashing uniforms, and comings and goings with great pomp and ceremony infuriated the president of our conference beyond measure and he had to be restrained from cancelling it on the spot.

Fortunately our own rooms had been safeguarded; I myself slept in great comfort during all the Ruritarian nonsense of the assembled heads of state – for this I was grateful to Captain Shaw and our Secretariat. I suspect they benefited from the influence of a PR person employed by the Togotese Minister of Information. He tried to get us to arrange a State Visit for the President to London. While we had an excellent dinner and were favoured in matters of accommodation, I don't think it was worth it. He was a species of Englishman and I can safely say I have seldom met such a frightful creep.

The President made a habit of summoning delegates to meet him at 5 o'clock in the morning. Happily, the acting chairman of the British group was a tough north countryman, Ted Garret, MP for one of the Newcastle constituencies. He informed the President's Emissary that we were here at an IPU conference and that he would be happy to attend only if his conference work allowed. The whole thing was ludicrous. It is on the whole beneficial to have the pseudo parliaments of often brutal dictatorships in the IPU, but the holding of the conference in Togo only served to increase the prestige of the President. Far from showing the desirability of real parliamentary government to the unfortunate members of the Togo parliament, they realised that their President was all powerful – able to summon the representatives of important western democracies from their beds at twenty minutes notice, to turn the President of the IPU out of his long-booked hotel, and to keep the whole conference waiting for nearly an hour before subjecting it to a Nuremberg-like display of his greatness. His grossly discourteous treatment of the delegates cannot be excused by saying 'This is Africa'. Let us be against such visits. The President was still in power in 1993, despite various efforts to get rid of him.

The conference itself showed some signs of improvement. John Gorst and I managed to help draft a fairly practical resolution on famine. The drafting committee was well composed with sensible people from the Third World. Senegal, India and even Cuba were reasonable. Our only trouble came from an Australian woman, but after initial courtesy we beat her down with true chauvinistic piggery. In the main committee an attempt by Algeria to insert the old canard that the famine was entirely due to the colonial era was well beaten. The reputation which the Ten Plus (an internal association of Western democracies) and the British delegation built up for their temperate approach and language was badly marred by a dreadful speech from Andrew Faulds, a Labour MP and former actor. It was worthy of the worst efforts of a delegate from North Korea or Democratic Yemen and without doubt contributed to the removal of a hard won phrase in the political resolution, which for the first time would have conceded the right of Israel to exist as a nation alongside a Palestinian state. Its removal was a source of deep disappointment to the Secretary General and many others.

The series of lunches initiated by the British group were successfully repeated in the case of the Irish lunch. The Russian lunch (the first one) went very well, until it was again spoilt by the intervention of Mr Faulds with a lecture on Afghanistan to our Russian guests. I hope and believe that the harm he did was smoothed over but I also thought that the interests of the IPU would be well served if he had no further opportunity to participate in the furtherance of peace and goodwill.

By way of contrast, the conference held in Seoul in South Korea was organised to the last detail and most impressive. We were aware that behind the energy and efficiency there was little parliamentary democracy, but nevertheless it drove home that the Pacific Rim was on the march and would be immensely powerful in thirty years time.

The Centenary Conference in 1989 was held in London as the United Kingdom was one of the two founder nations. For once, the Treasury opened their coffers to a reasonable extent. The Queen headed an immensely impressive and moving opening ceremony for delegates from all over the world in Westminster Hall, with its great hammer beam roof and the trumpeters in the great window, so beautifully placed by Barry when the Palace of Westminster was rebuilt. It gave an excellent start to the conference. At the other end of the scale, we organised 'a piss-up in a brewery'. An admirable party was held in a great brewery in the City, which again, on a different level, was voted a tremendous success. We had all the fun of the fair – jugglers and so on – and a fitting climax to 100 years of parliamentary co-operation.

The Spring Conference of the Inter Parliamentary Union in 1994 was held in Paris. Because the Labour Party was not co-operating with the Government on Commons business matters, no MPs could attend, except for the Chairman, John Ward, who rushed in and out, eventually coming back on Friday for the finish of the Conference on Saturday. The gap was filled by peers, led by David Montgomery, with myself as deputy, Nora David, Magnam Desai, Heather Brigstock and Jamie Lindsay. We put up at the Hilton Hotel at exorbitant cost and had a thoroughly enjoyable week.

We also had two clerks, John Sweetman from the House of Commons and Michael Davies from the House of Lords, both great assets socially as well as for their expertise. The main subjects were regional co-operation with the United Nations and a rather specialised pollution subject, 'Waste Material'. The main debate on the UN gave an opportunity for me to criticise the total failure of Europe to unite over the slaughter in Bosnia. This was a recurrent theme amongst the Parliamentarians present, except, of course, for the Serbs. The only piece of organisation we did not like in Paris was the reception given by the City of Paris, the Mayor being Jacques Chirac, who asked us for 7.30 p.m., kept 1,000 delegates waiting without a drink while he drank with the nobs, then made a speech lasting half an hour with interpretation. The speech was purely for public consumption in France as he was a Presidential candidate. I did not push forward to shake his hand after the speeches, as I thought it was a disgraceful way for a host to behave.

CHAPTER 21

The Loss of Lindsay

IN THE SPRING OF 1985, Lindsay and I went to Cyprus on a mixture of business and holiday, and enjoyed the trip. But she didn't look 100 per cent when we got home and I urged her to have a check-up. She refused. I was rather concerned all summer, and before we went to Bulgaria as part of a delegation she promised to go see the doctor on our return. Our friends Geoff and Pat Tordoff were the other representatives from the Lords and for a few days we had an interesting and enjoyable time. But halfway through the trip, Lindsay was very tired and ill one night. She recovered a little in the morning and refused to see a Bulgarian doctor. We nursed her carefully through the rest of the trip and went for tests for her obvious anaemia when we got home. The test showed a very low count of red corpuscles. That could be cured by blood transfusions, but the doctor wanted a biopsy of the bone marrow to make sure.

When Dr Cruickshank brought the results out, they showed a positive reaction to leukaemia. It was a great shock and Lindsay burst into a storm of weeping, quickly recovered and, with wonderful courage, started to cope with the sort of treatment we would seek. I found that the unit in Ninewells, Dundee, was one of the best in the country and she went into Ninewells to Ward 7 under Dr Hepplestone. She had a nice small room which was soon covered with cards from wellwishers and the treatment started, with the whole family hoping for a cure or remission.

She knew how ill she was, but she too was hopeful at this time. Her ambition was to see her home again, and she spoke longingly of her return to Benshie. The course of treatment did not give the hoped for result but we still had hopes of further measures. I think by this time Lindsay knew she was dying and indeed, John Stevenson, our Minister, told me afterwards she did know. Young doctors suggested she go to Intensive Care for treatment that would help her breathing and she consented, bravely saying we must try everything. I went with her and stayed most of the night, thoroughly disapproving of the whole attitude in the section. In the morning, I insisted she return to her room and when the specialist, who had been away the previous day, returned, he said she should not have been moved. When Lindsay was wheeled into her room, which had become 'home' to her, her face lit up with pleasure. By this time we were all worried about her, and one of the family was always at her bedside, except Lindsay Junior, who was pregnant with Lizzie Lindsay. Lindsay Senior insisted that she have proper rest.

All this time Lindsay had never despaired. But now she did and I could not comfort her.

Diana did, and sat talking to her until she regained her marvellous courage and acceptance. She fell asleep and the next day I was summoned from next door as she was sinking, and she died peacefully in her sleep. We took her home and she was laid in our bedroom until the funeral. People on the farm, and indeed in the Parish, were shocked by her death as she was only a young sixty-four. The Old Parish Church in Kirriemuir was full and the service was very moving. Many people came to the cemetery on the hill above the town, where her grave looks over Strathmore and Benshie is clearly in view.

All the family were devastated, but I had terrific support from all my daughters. Going through the routine of the funeral and seeing that all was done fittingly for Lindsay was in itself a great help in the first days and occupied the mind. A lot has been written about grief and some of it is a comfort to the stricken. In my case, work and routine was helpful but I knew I would recover. What hit me between the eyes was that Lindsay was gone – long before her time – and would never again enjoy the things she loved. I wrote long laments and recollections of her and our life together. I am not a religious man, but I wanted desperately to believe we would meet again. I wrote a little poem in child-prayer form:

> Jesus Tender Shepherd
> Keep her
> Safe and sure
> Through dark and light
> Keep her
> Till again I meet her
> In the promised after life.

Gradually the pain eased and my family were the greatest support, as I hope I was to them. Friends were very helpful and I was busy. David

Steel, on the suggestion of Stephen Ross, MP for the Isle of Wight, appointed me a member of the Parliamentary Assembly of the Council of Europe and of the Western European Union. This was new territory and I greatly enjoyed Strasbourg, Paris, and interesting new work. I had eleven years in Europe and am grateful to David for appointing me.

In the late summer of 1986, I was gloomily working in my office at Benshie when I was told I had a visitor. In came Jacqui Lane, widow of my old partner in Tongue and John O'Groats and indeed a partner herself in the venture. She lifted the gloom and the following year we saw a great deal of each other and by the autumn of 1987 had decided to marry. This showed good sense on my part. Our wedding was held in the Crypt of the House of Commons in April 1988. Our children were all pleased. I am still grateful for my good sense and good fortune as I write this in 2003.

CHAPTER 22

The Council of Europe

CARL AHRENS was in the German Navy in World War II. He had been in and out of Benghazi, a main supply port for Rommel, where we often bombed the ships in the harbour during my time in the RAF. So when we met in Strasbourg at the Council of Europe more than forty years on, I apologised for missing him! He accepted my apology!! A lawyer and the head of the Socialist Group, he was a genuine bulwark of democracy in West Germany and we fraternised happily. The German delegation was able and one could admire the hard work they put in.

The Council of Europe was the first European body formed after the Second War. It has no governmental function, apart from the legal power vested in the Court of Human Rights. It is, however, a very important meeting place for European Members of Parliament and was certainly recognised as such by the East European countries when they were released from bondage in 1989. Indeed, Russia itself was very keen to join and in spite of doubts, was allowed in, as the members thought the cause of human rights could be advanced faster with Russia inside than as a rejected suitor.

The Headquarters is in Strasbourg, in a building shared with the European Parliament. Of course, Jacqui was back in her native land. She made many friends in Council circles but she ruined my already bad French. When in doubt I said, 'Jacqui, ask him, tell him.' My French got worse but as English is by far the most commonly spoken language one could get by or, indeed, get on very well. French is the other official language of the Council of Europe, so Jacqui was able to make contact with couples from a number of different countries and this was very useful. She was particularly popular with the Turks for some reason.

We stayed mainly in a small hotel, Le Cruche d'Or, run by a Monsieur and Madame Zimmer. There was no lift, and four storeys. The exercise was beneficial. The restaurant was excellent. He was a good chef and she ran a 40-cover restaurant by herself with great competence and charm. They had, of course, some help for cleaning but, on their own, kept a full restaurant fed and happy. Madame was, in addition, a very good-looking woman and smart.

I enjoyed the mixture of nationalities and got on very well with most people. But I cannot say I thought much of the Greek Cypriots. They spoke constantly of the Turkish 'invasion' and the evils of separation – never a word of the British soldiers they killed, nor the ethnic cleansing of Turks from Greek villages, nor of the fact that the partition was brought about by their attempt to put the whole island under Greek rule. I much preferred the straightforward Turks, who didn't pretend to be angels.

Initially, I was put on the Migration Committee and was made Raporteur of a sub-committee investigating the handling of asylum seekers at international airports. The problems are with us today. Many people in poor countries would like to escape to the developed world where even a menial job gives a standard of life unattainable in their own country (and who can blame them?). By international agreement, European countries will give asylum to those refugees who go in fear of their lives and their liberty in war zones and oppressive dictator states. The problem is to distinguish the genuine asylum seeker from the economic refugee.

As always, racketeers made a deal of money advising economic refugees how to deceive the receiving countries and in many cases, took all the money from sales of their assets. The receiving countries tried various devices to stem the flow. Britain fined airlines that landed people without papers. The French tried to say that certain areas of international airports such as Charles de Gaulle were not part of France and sent the refugees straight back. They were not pleased with me when I described this as lowdown deceit. It was true that the racketeers picked the countries which were easier to penetrate. In my report I did suggest that as the genuine areas of danger of persecution are well known, international camps could be set up in neighbouring countries, and those in genuine danger could be certified as such, before boarding the aircraft. I know the obvious difficulties but when you look at the waiting lists today, it might help.

I moved to the Agricultural Committee, where my expertise was useful and I visited Albania, Bulgaria, Rumania, Hungary and Poland during the Soviet period. In the good lands I found that agriculture under the large so-called 'Co-operative System' was well done, with good crops being harvested. The farms were generally over-manned but the system was working and the market in the Soviet Union itself took all their surplus grain. On the big collective farms nursery schools, housing for retired workers and many other social services were part of the farm set-up. I don't mean to suggest that this was a rural paradise – far from it – corruption and incompetence were rife and many people were dissatisfied. What I do suggest was that our advice on a quick dash for a free market system caused a great deal of harm and distress.

After the collapse of the Eastern Block, I went back to an area in Hungary that had been particularly impressive. It was on good land, south of Budapest, and both arable and stock were well managed and a pleasure to inspect. Two years later the place was a mess, large areas had not been sown and the farmers were unhappy. They had never had financial responsibilities and with the loss of their best market money ran out. They could not buy seed or even manure, if they could find it. They simply weren't ready for the market system.

I attended the Spring Meeting of the Council of Europe in Warsaw in May 1994 in order to present my report on a previous colloquy on the privatisation of state agriculture in Eastern Europe, mainly about Polish agriculture. I presented this report on the morning of Wednesday 18th and it was passed unanimously by a standing committee and the chairman expressed his congratulations to me, I think quite sincerely, although normally everyone, however much they disapprove of a report, starts off by congratulating the reporter.

This, however, was not the main purpose of the visit. I wanted to follow up the report with a study of how the privatisation of the state farms was progressing in Poland. To this end, I contacted Dr Andrzej Malinowski through the Directory and tried the Foreign Office and the Embassy there. The Embassy were not particularly helpful and suggested nothing, but Dr Malinowski put me in touch with the agency handling the privatisation of the state farms in Poland. State farms account for about 20 per cent of the land, the rest being in small farms. There is no doubt at all that the high percentage of small farms and the Catholic Church had a terrific unifying effect on the people of Poland, and without doubt kept the worst features of Communism at bay, giving a background against which Lech Walesa was able to organise the shipyards and bring democracy back to Poland.

The 20 per cent under state farms included much of the best land in Poland and was organised in units which were really too large for efficient working. They not only farmed the land, but they also in many cases organised the packaging and distribution of the goods, as well as running nursery schools and building houses for both workers and retired workers, so that you had cases of 10,000 hectares of land organised more or less like a self-contained community.

The farms were completely over staffed in Western terms, but they did provide security and work, at a fairly low level of income. Initially, under pressure from Western economic advisers, the Polish government simply made the state farms financially independent and simultaneously withdrew the subsidies on food which had enabled the elderly population to live reasonably well and to buy the meat produced on the farms. At the same time, the Russian market disappeared as the former Soviet Union was no longer able to pay, with the result that there was a slump in price.

The management committees of these state farms, and the so called co-operatives, had never been subject to financial discipline in their lives, with the result that the only roads open to them were bankruptcy or cutting their costs. They did not know how to cut costs and anyhow were providing a social service as well as farming. The result was a catastrophic fall in production, with land lying idle for want of the money to buy fertiliser, fuel or seeds. The new agency which came into being has taken a grip of the situation, but in very difficult circumstances. They have large assets, but no money to develop them, so they are in the position of a factor or agent on a large British estate with incompetent tenants and big past obligations.

They are now splitting the big farms into workable sizes, from 500 to 1,000 hectares, and leasing them to competent groups of tenants, both foreign and Polish. They are willing to sell, but the reason for selling is to raise money in order to run the rest of their estate properly. The practice is to ask for tenders from local groups who can raise the capital to farm the land, and to then let the land to the best and most practical offerer. Where they have no offers from reasonable people, they are selecting groups and giving them management contracts, whereby they can in the future assess their competence and when they have the money, lend them the capital to farm the land.

I spent a day with a former diplomat, Maciej Lewandowski, an adviser of the agency. He picked me up at 9 o'clock and we set off by car. They have, very sensibly, split the land into estates and set up a management body in each area. We motored south for about 150 kilometres and looked at fish farming in the lakes and at a big, not yet privatised, state farm. I found Mr Lewandowski very interesting, a very able young man. When we got to our destination, we met the chairman of the Union of Fishermen who fished the lakes and who fed and stocked them and the chief of the estate in that part of the world, who was a lawyer. Over lunch and, needless to say, vodka, we had a very good discussion and I was much impressed by the quality of the local people. They talked in very practical terms and they talked about the quality of their possible tenants and their training. This appeared to me to be the right way to start.

After lunch we went into the farm and were shown round by the present chief. He had been there for twenty-odd years. They were splitting this farm up into a number of projects and the head chap, along with a consortium, was bidding for the pig farming enterprise with enough ground to grow the feed for the pigs. This was a modern, well-managed piggery with over 1,000 sows.

We were entertained in the mansion which had been the centre of the estate, and I was horrified to see more food being laid out. After another tour, we had more vodka and then sat down to a further meal, which of course, we could not refuse. While the head man appeared to me to be a typical Communist boss of the enterprise, it also appeared to me that he would be well able to adjust to financial responsibility and the chances were that he and his group would get the pig enterprise. They were in the process of setting up a separate housing trust for the 400 or 500 houses they had, many of them housing retired workers on the farm, and separating the vodka distillery and the sheep and dairy part of the enterprise. They had to close down the kindergarten which they were running and this had yet to be taken over by the local authority. Their problems were obviously very large, but I thought that the agency was tackling them in the right way.

We drove back then to Warsaw and I had further long chats with Mr Lewandowski. Next day I went to see Mr Adam Tanski, the President of the agency, and had a long and interesting chat with him. It was quite obvious that what they wanted me to do was to get as much British money into farming as possible. They still have a traditional dislike of Germans occupying Polish land, but they have great interest from both Holland and Denmark and also from Britain. Two young Scots I know rented a large area at that time and were able to pay decent wages for the area, but still, in relation to the price of a ton of barley, labour was very cheap. They had to resort to all sorts of devices to get seed and manure, for example hiring two lorries and driving them into West Germany to buy and collect fertiliser. It was a most useful and illuminating visit and I promised I would do my best and keep up the contacts. Jacqui and I stayed in great comfort in the Bristol Hotel, which was not quite as expensive as I thought it was going to be. Our last afternoon was most enjoyable – we simply relaxed and had a very good dinner in the hotel at night.

In Albania, the agricultural situation was quite extraordinary. The peasants, who had been savagely oppressed under the worst Communist regime in Europe, simply took over the land and split it into family units. There had been a significant wine producing area but the Government was forced to break it up and restore the land to the original farmers who used the vineyards to graze their cattle. They knew little about running small farms and the agricultural advisory service had great difficulty in putting over good practice. I advised them to pick a farmer who was making money and use his farm as a demonstration unit.

I stayed on the Council of Europe until 1998. Subsequently, I mainly concentrated on Committee work, leaving the front bench to younger members. I had liked my work in Strasbourg.

The Future of the House of Lords

I continue to attend the House of Lords where I pursue my various interests from the back benches. I have been a member of the executive of the Inter-Parliamentary Union for 25 years. I am a member of the Commonwealth Association and other Associations in the House. I always attend question time and put in my word when I think I have something relevant to say. I greatly enjoy the House but I must say at the age of 84 that I consider there are far too many old people like myself still there. It is true that we sometimes have something relevant to say but in the main we are not entirely up to date on our subjects. Certainly for myself I know that many practices in farming today are not familiar to me. As an example I rang an old friend to get a bag of potato manure for my croquet lawn. He suggested I must have a big lawn as potato manure was now sold in ton bags. However as long as my fare is paid and reasonable allowances are available I will continue to go there.

The answer must be retirement age backed by a pension reflecting the number of years served. A Peer should be able to retire at 75 and accept compulsory retirement at 80. They should be able to attend debates and speak if they wish but would not vote or put down motions or questions. They would not receive allowances for travel or attendance but would have their pension. Many Peers would take the pension and the House would lose its geriatric look as well as taking in members with up to date experience.

The House of Lords must be an appointed House: an elected one would be a replica of and a rival to the Commons, which must always have the last word. Political Peers should be appointed by the parties according to their vote in the country, not by the number of members in the Commons. Independent Peers should be appointed by an independent committee (the present committee is working well).

Even if illogically composed the House of Lords has done good work over the years and can do even better in the future, improving ill thought out legislations for the benefit of the electors and indeed introducing helpful measures.

The House of Commons needs reform by the introduction of a fair system of voting which would reflect the value of the member as well as the support for the party.

The whole family outside the Portland Arms in Lybster, Caithness.

At the count in 1964 – Mackie complacent, knowing he had won.

The Liberal MPs in 1965 – (from left) David Steel, Hooson, our hostess Steena Robson, Mackie, Lubbock, Mackenzie, Grimond, Johnston and Thorpe.

Installation ceremony in the House of Lords, 1974 – Mackie not entirely at ease in ludicrous costume.

At a ploughing match during the 1979 European election.

Visit of Icelandic IPU delegation to Benshie.

Lord Rhodes' delegation to China in 1981. Lord Rhodes and former Labour Chief Whip Pat Llewelyn-Davies are flanking the number three in the Chinese heirarchy.

With the leaders of a Russian delegation and a top German cartoonist in Bonn after Chernobyl.

Bulgaria 1985 with Lord and Lady Tordoff and our Bulgarian guides and interpreter.

Lindsay with grand-daughter Sunnifa in Tomintoul.

Addressing the Council of Europe in Strasbourg – note the empty seats!

*Supporters pulling carriage over Tay Bridge after election
as Rector of Dundee University.*

Jacqui – about to put her feet up in Parliament House, Ottawa.

Jacqui in Beijing.

With Jacqui in the garden at Cortachy House.

CHAPTER 23

The Sale of Benshie

IN 1985, WHEN I WAS 66, Lindsay and I had decided that I should retire from farming and concentrate on my work in the House of Lords and that we would see more of the world. I had sold to and leased back the farm from a friend who wanted it as a secure trust for his younger son. The son was now a married man and anxious to realise his capital. Farms were fetching a good price, and we made a bargain on how the money would be split. The sale arrangements were well advanced when Lindsay took ill and, of course, everything was cancelled.

After she died, I altered my plans as the routine of farming in my home for forty years was an anchor for all the family. After Jacqui and I got married we settled down in Benshie, and Jacqui made a terrific job of taking on Lindsay's house, and our friends, and the people on the farm. It must have been a great strain, but she coped so well that Ruby who had been our cook for eighteen years still comes to us for a few hours a week in her retirement.

In 1989 (my seventieth year), a friend who was an estate agent wrote to me saying he had a client who would like to buy Benshie. I checked with my young landlord and, although land prices had declined, he was keen to sell. I thought that as I had neither sons nor daughters in the farming business, I would like to concentrate on my work in the House of Lords. The farm was sold, and the staff who were retiring bought or rented houses. The manager, Graham Scrymgeour, the head fruitman, Angus Robbie, and Joe Milne, the stockman, stayed on with the new owner. Bob Spalding bought a house in Kirriemuir near the Golf Course, Harry Reith bought one near Forfar and Ruby rented one in Kirriemuir. Jacqui and I couldn't find a house we wanted to buy, so we rented Cortachy House from Lord Airlie. Cortachy House is smack in the middle of Cortachy Castle's policies, the glorious trees of the American Garden are over the garden wall, and the fairy-tale castle, 300 yards away, can be glimpsed through the trees. It is difficult to buy a house half as nice.

After eight years, however, we realised that we needed a smaller, comfortable house with some neighbours. In the hamlet of Oathlaw we found a house standing in about an acre, totally enclosed by high hedges and with an acre of birch wood behind. The house needed a great deal done to it, but Jacqui has transformed it and we have now been here for five years. We have found Oathlaw relaxing and we have good neighbours. We have a good local pub at Finavon and can put up children and grandchildren there if we are having a party. Jacqui has four children and seven grandchildren, I have three daughters and seven granddaughters. We like them and indeed admire them and enjoy seeing them. We enjoy our small, warm house. Jacqui looks after the garden and I look after the cellar.

Index